COMPUTER ENGINEERING DIPLOMA & ENGINEERING MCQ

MANOJ DOLE

Made with ❤ on the Notion Press Platform
www.notionpress.com

Contents

Foreword

Computer Engineering Diploma & Engineering MCQ is a Book for Computer Engineering Course, Revised Syllabus, It contains objective questions with underlined & bold correct answers MCQ covering all topics including all about the latest & Important about Introduction to computer concepts, Concepts of electrical and electronics engineering, Programming using C , Digital , Basic electronics , Programming with C , Basic Computer Skills , Multimedia , Applied Science, Engineering Physics, Engineering Chemistry Computer Organization, OOP with C++ Data Structures Using C Database , Management System, Computer Networks, Operating System, Data Structures , Software Engineering, PC Hardware and Networking ,Graphic User Interface , Web Designing , Linux , Software Testing Programming with java, Network Security and Management, Web Programming, Mobile Computing, Programming with java , Software Testing , Web Programming , Network Security, computer peripherals, internal components, basic DOS commands, Windows and Linux interface and its related software installation. MS Office word document, excel sheet and power point presentation, database with MS Access. network system of an organization. internet browser basic static webpage using HTML. JavaScript and dynamic webpage and hosting technique in a registered domain. VBA to create & edit various types of macros in MS Excel and to develop user form using VBA. accounting software Tally. E-commerce system and E-commerce websites. cyber crimes secure information from Internet by cyber security concept.

We add new question answers with each new version. Please email us in case of any errors/omissions. This is arguably the largest and best e-Book for All engineering multiple choice questions and answers.

As a student you can use it for your exam prep. This Book is also useful for professors to refresh material.

Preface

This book may be purchased for educational, business, or sales promotional use. Online edition is also available for this title. For more information, contact our corporate/institutional sales department: [+919921582799] or [manojdole1@gmail.com]

While every precaution has been taken in the preparation of this book, the publisher and authors assume no responsibility for errors or omissions, or for damages resulting from the use of the information contained herein.

About the Author

MANOJ DOLE is an Engineer from reputed University. He is currently working with Government Industrial Training- Institute as a lecturer from last 12 Years. His interest include- Engineering Training Material, Invention & Engineering Practical- Knowledge etc.

CHAPTER ONE

Computer Engineering Theory

Download App | Online Test Exam | ITI Books | AutoCAD CAM | JOB & Apprentice

Online Theory | Computer Course | Trading Course | CNC Course | MSCIT Course

Shopping Business | Internet Business | Web Designing | Online Services | Top Sportsmans

Indian Army | Freedom Fighters | Top Scientists | Social Reformers | Motivational Speaker

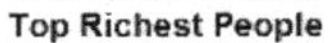

Top Richest People

Join WhatsApp Group

Join Facebook Group

Like Facebook Page

PAN / Adhar / Licence Passport

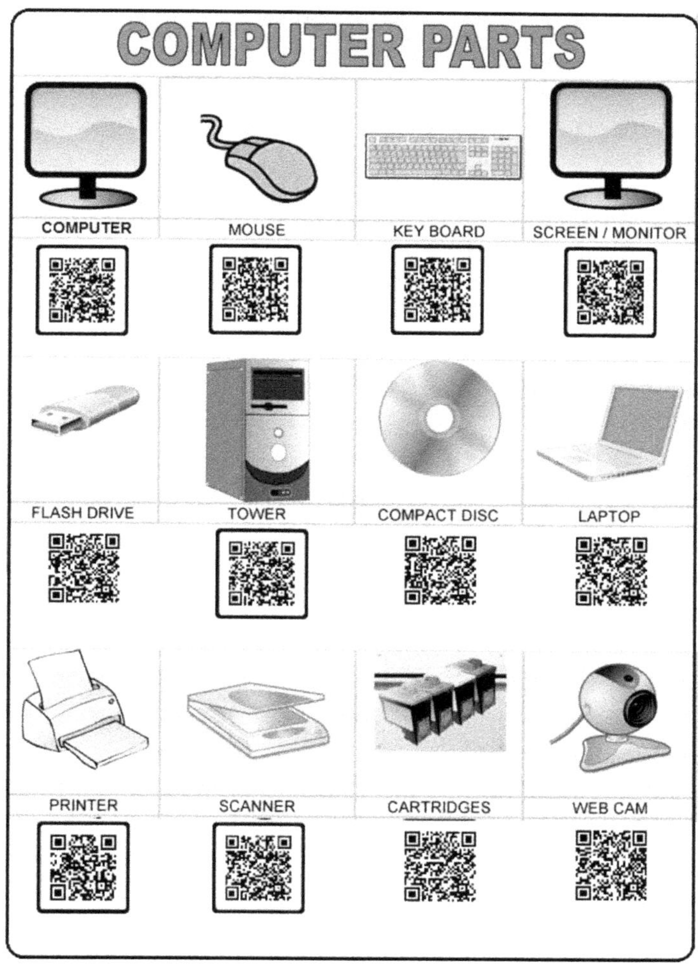
COMPUTER PARTS
COMPUTER
MOUSE
KEY BOARD
SCREEN / MONITOR
FLASH DRIVE
TOWER
COMPACT DISC
LAPTOP
PRINTER
SCANNER
CARTRIDGES
WEB CAM

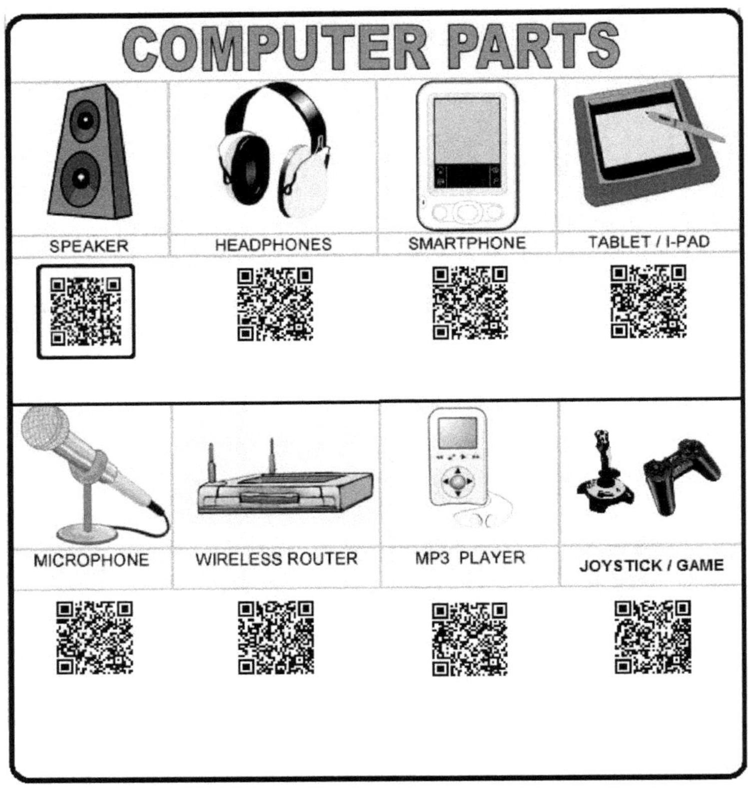
COMPUTER PARTS
SPEAKER
HEADPHONES
SMARTPHONE
TABLET / I-PAD
MICROPHONE
WIRELESS ROUTER
MP3 PLAYER
JOYSTICK / GAME

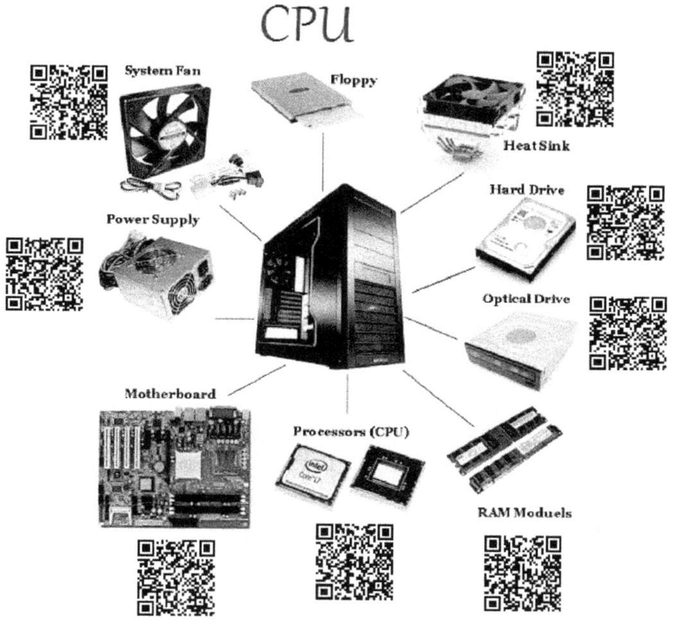

Computer CPU Hardware Components

Motherboard Hardware Components

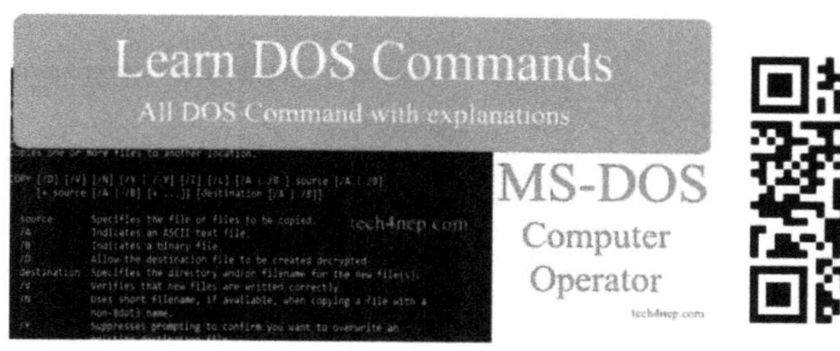

Excel Basic Functions

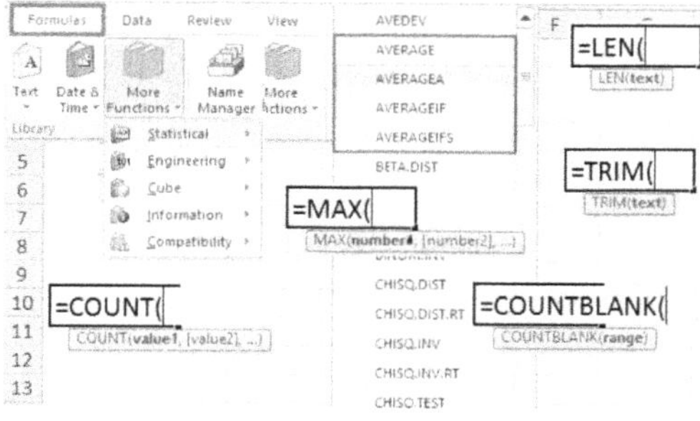

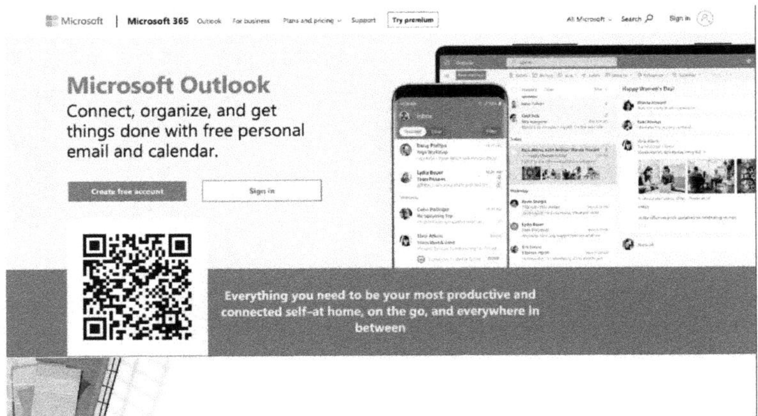
Microsoft | Microsoft 365
Try premium
Microsoft Outlook
Connect, organize, and get things done with free personal email and calendar.
Create free account
Sign in
Everything you need to be your most productive and connected self-at home, on the go, and everywhere in between

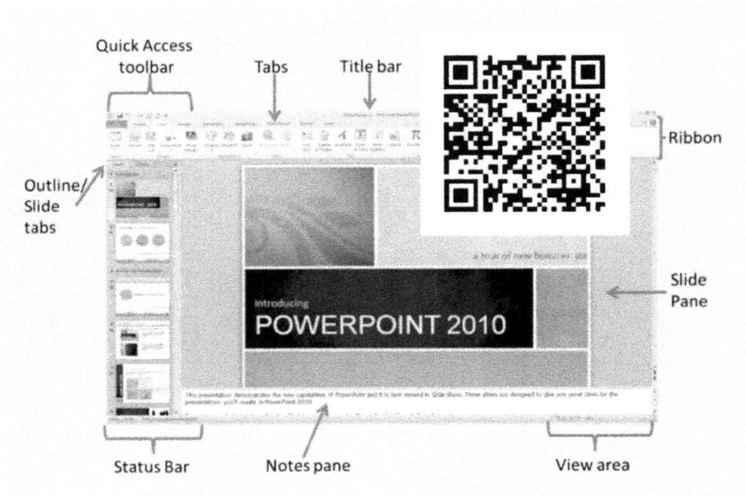
Quick Access toolbar
Tabs
Title bar
Ribbon
Outline/ Slide tabs
Introducing
POWERPOINT 2010
Slide Pane
Status Bar
Notes pane
View area

MS Paint

Microsoft
FEATURES OF
MS WORD
IN HINDI
• WHAT IS MS WORD
• HISTORY OF MS WORD
• FEATURES OF MS WORD

CDBurnerXP
Data disc
Video DVD
Audio disc
Burn ISO image
Copy or grab disc
Erase disc
OK
Exit

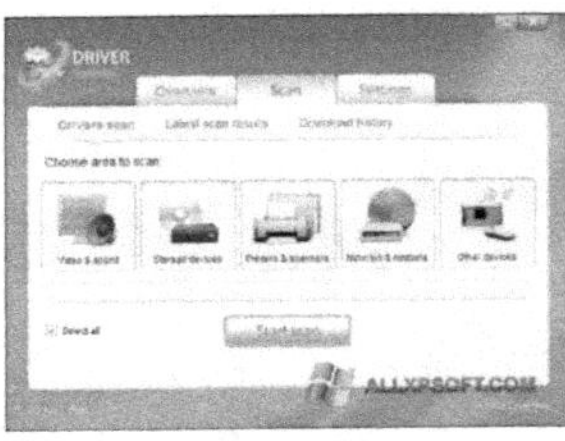
DRIVER
ALLXPSOFT.COM

Top Linux OS
debian
ZORIN OS
KALI

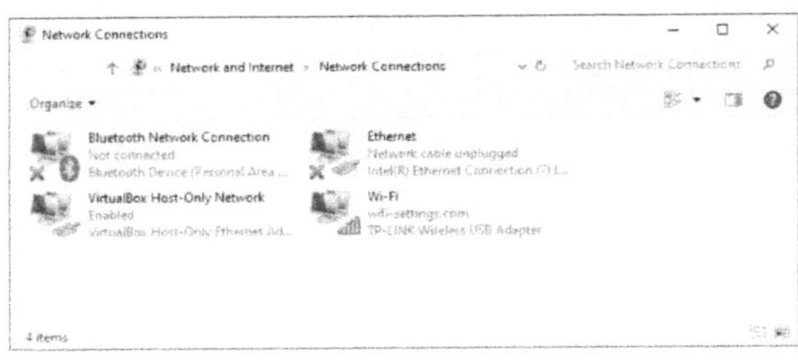
Network Connections
Network and Internet
Network Connections
Organize
Bluetooth Network Connection
Not connected
Ethernet
Network cable unplugged
VirtualBox Host-Only Network
Enabled
Wi-Fi
wifi-settings.com
TP-LINK Wireless USB Adapter
4 items

Software Installation

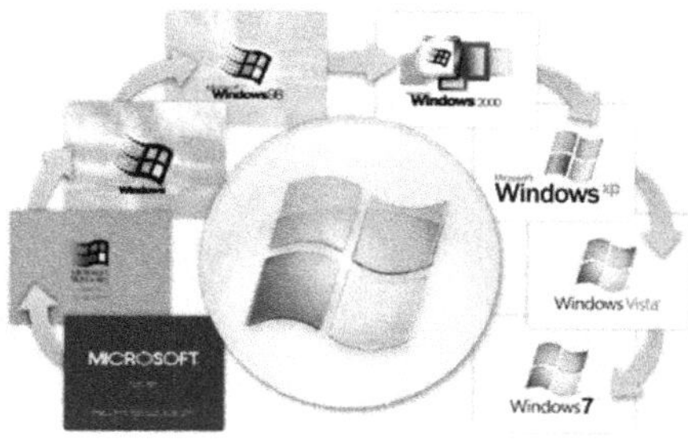

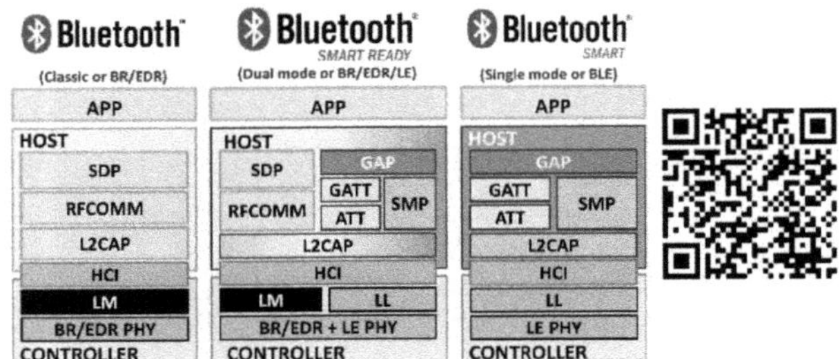
Bluetooth
(Classic or BR/EDR)
Bluetooth
SMART READY
(Dual mode or BR/EDR/LE)
Bluetooth
SMART
(Single mode or BLE)
APP
HOST
SDP
RFCOMM
L2CAP
HCI
LM
BR/EDR PHY
CONTROLLER
GAP
GATT
ATT
SMP
LL
BR/EDR + LE PHY
LE PHY

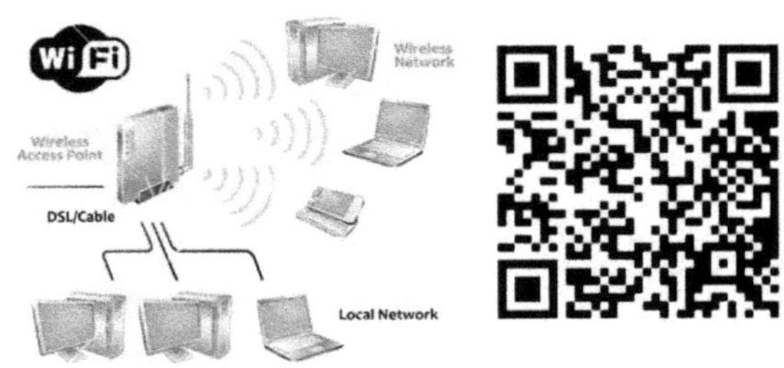
Wi Fi
Wireless Network
Wireless Access Point
DSL/Cable
Local Network

What is a Browser - Definition and

What is
Email?

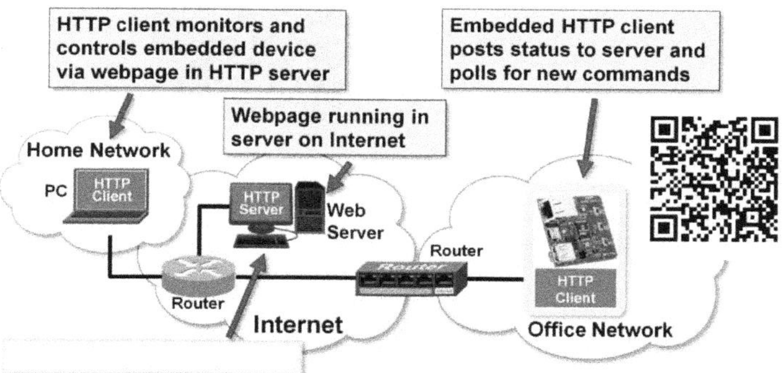
HTTP client monitors and
controls embedded device
via webpage in HTTP server
Embedded HTTP client
posts status to server and
polls for new commands
Webpage running in
server on Internet
Home Network
PC
HTTP
Client
HTTP
Server
Web
Server
Router
Router
Internet
HTTP
Client
Office Network

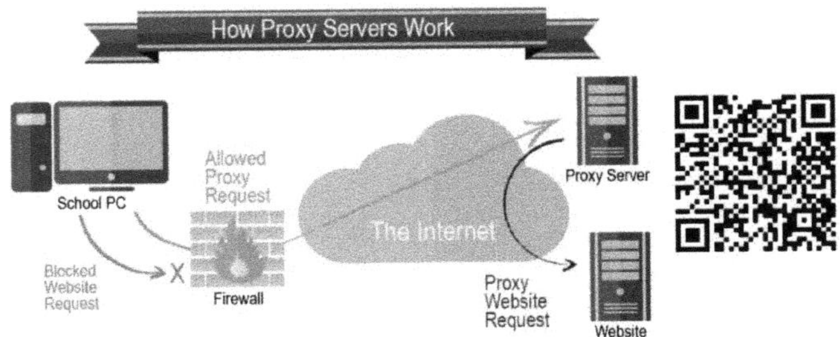

Full HTML & CSS Website

Domain-Name-System

Domain-Name-System

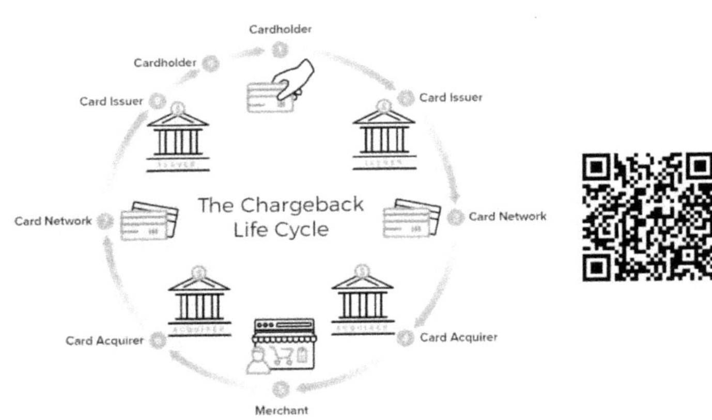
Cardholder
Cardholder
Card Issuer
Card Issuer
The Chargeback Life Cycle
Card Network
Card Network
Card Acquirer
Card Acquirer
Merchant

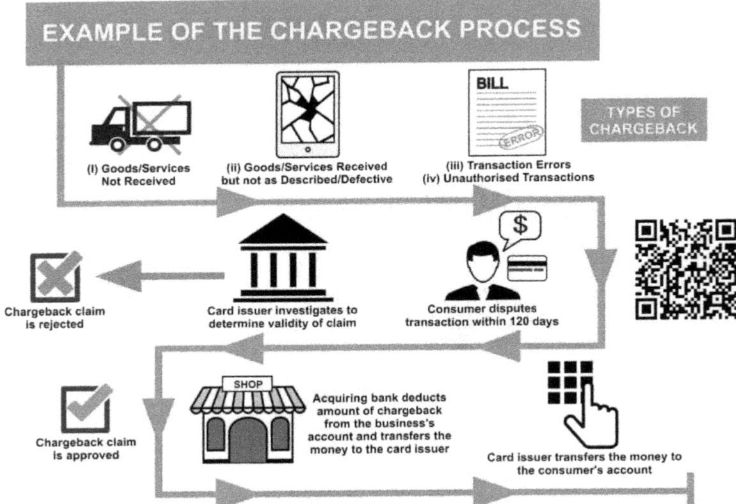
EXAMPLE OF THE CHARGEBACK PROCESS
TYPES OF CHARGEBACK
(I) Goods/Services Not Received
(ii) Goods/Services Received but not as Described/Defective
BILL
ERROR
(iii) Transaction Errors
(iv) Unauthorised Transactions
$
Chargeback claim is rejected
Card issuer investigates to determine validity of claim
Consumer disputes transaction within 120 days
SHOP
Chargeback claim is approved
Acquiring bank deducts amount of chargeback from the business's account and transfers the money to the card issuer
Card issuer transfers the money to the consumer's account

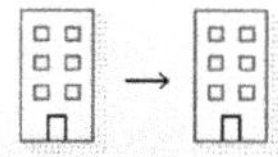

Business to business

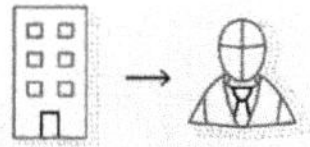

Business to consumer

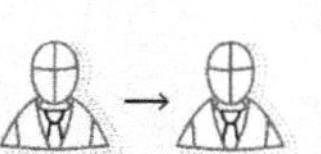

Consumer to consumer

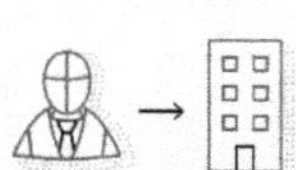

Consumer to business

Payment & Order Processing

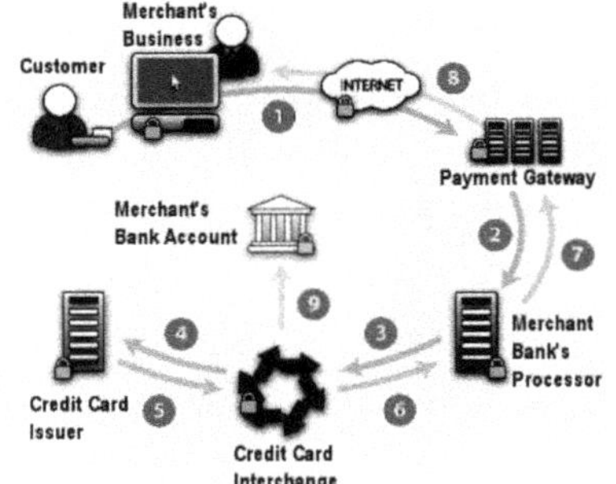

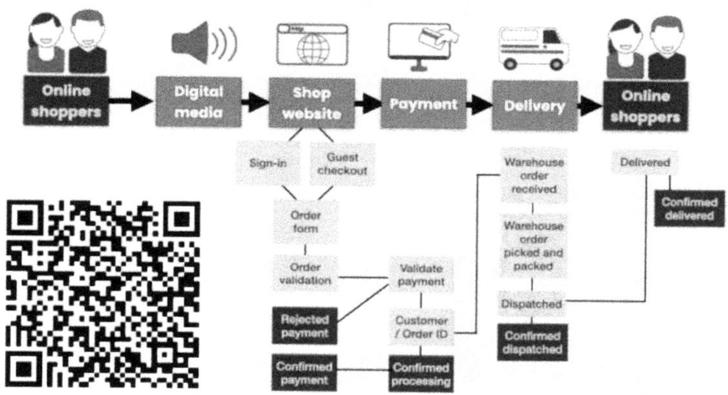
Order to delivery : ideal experience
Online shoppers
Digital media
Shop website
Payment
Delivery
Online shoppers
Sign-in
Guest checkout
Order form
Order validation
Validate payment
Rejected payment
Customer / Order ID
Confirmed payment
Confirmed processing
Warehouse order received
Warehouse order picked and packed
Dispatched
Confirmed dispatched
Delivered
Confirmed delivered

Top 8 Best Payment Gateways for Your Online Store
PayPal
Razorpay
stripe
Braintree
authorize.net
Paytm
instamojo
CC Avenue
PAYMENTS
$200

How payment gateways help you accept and send payments:

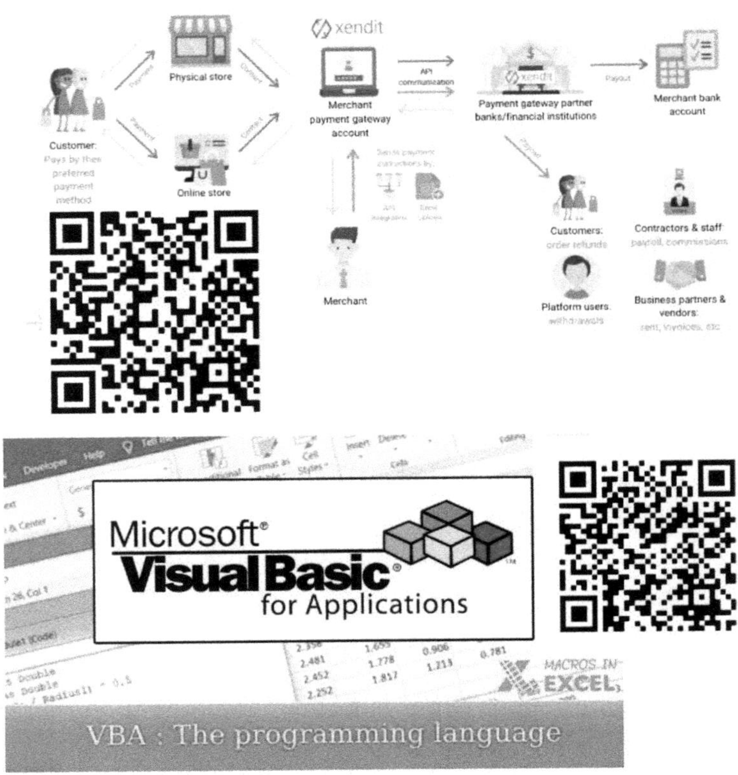

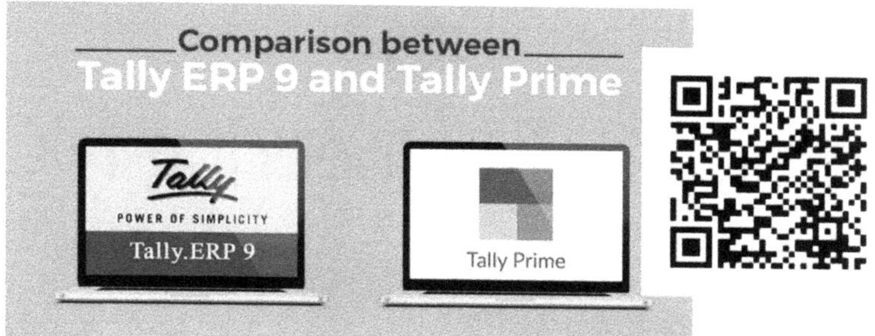
Comparison between
Tally ERP 9 and Tally Prime
Tally
POWER OF SIMPLICITY
Tally.ERP 9
Tally Prime

Social
Networking
Sites
SOCIAL MEDIA
MARKETING

CYBER SECURITY

CHAPTER TWO

Computer Engineering MCQ

1] ABC stands for --------------

A] Automatic Breathing Control

B] Automatic Blood Control

C] Airway Breathing Circulation

D] Automatic Blood Circulation

3] To put off"Class B" fire, the types of fire extinguisher used is ....

A] dry power

B] Carbon dioxide

C] Jet of water

D] Foam type

4] Which type of fire extinguisher is used to put off general fire?

A] Water type Extinguisher

B] Foam type Extinguisher

C] Dry chemical powder Extinguisher

D] Carbon dioxide (C02] Extinguisher

5] In case of bleeding, take treatment Of

D] cold 3" and rest

A] spray cold water

B] Bandage immediately -----.

B] Enquire about the accident thought treatment

6] in case of an accident, the victim should im

A] Asked to take rest

C] Attended immediately

D] leave him

7] First aid is given to an injured or ill person primarily....

A] Save life

B] Prevent further deterioration of the muff's

C] Give best possible comfort

D] All of these

Q.1. Which of the following is the biggest unit of memory?

A] Gigabytes.

B] bytes.

C] Megabytes.

D] Kilobytes.

Q.2. The primary purpose of software is to turn data into.

A] Website.

B] Infromation.

C] Programs.

D] Objects.

Q.3. GUI Stands for

A] Graphical User Interface.

B] Greater User Interface.

C] Graphical Union Interface.

D] Graphical User Intereat.

Q.4. Key board keys that have arrows on them are called -

A] Function Keys.

B] Navigation Keys.

C] Typewriter Keys.

D] Special purpose keys.

Q.5. ASSCII, EBCDIC and Unicode are examples of Application Software's

A] True.

B] False.

Q.6. The easiest way to access any part of the screen in the windows operating system is using the.

A] Key Board.

B] Rat.

C] Mouse.

D]] Joystick.

Q.7. A software is also called as a

A] Procedure.

B] Data.

C] Programs.

D] Information.

Q.8. Back programs make copies of the files to be used in case the original files are damaged or lost.

A] True.

B] False.

Q.9. Microprocessor is often called as CPU

A] True.

B] False.

Q.10. .... Utility identifies unnecessary files on the hard disk and erases them based on users command.

A] Backup.

B] File Compression.

C] Uninstall Programs.

D]] Disk Clean up.

Q.11. This type of software is designs to help you be more productive tasks, and is widely used in nearly every disc live and occupation.

A] Communication Software.

B] Utility Software.

C] Basic Application Software.

D] System Software.

Q.12. Minicomputers are also known as.

A] Mid Range Computers.

B] Personal Digital Computers.

C] Mainframe Computers.

D] Laptop Computers.

Q.13. Which of the following device is used to play fast games on a computers.

A] Touch Surface.

B] Touch Screen.2

C] Track Ball.

D] Joystick.

Q.14. Which of the following would not be considered as portable computer.

A] Desktop Computer.

B] Note book computer.

C] Personal Digital Assistant.

D] None of these.

Q.15. Headphone is a typical output device.

A] True.

B] False.

Q.16. Uninstall programs help us to remove unwanted programs installed in the computer.

A] True.

B] False.

Q.17. The capacity of a storage device is usually measured in terms of bytes.

A] True.

B] False.

Q.18. Capacity of the storage device is usually measured in terms of meter.

A] True.

B] False.

Q.19............. is a pointing device.

A] Mouse.

B] Printer.

C] Scanner.

D] Keyboard.

Q.20. The keyboards keys that are labelled F1, F2 and so on are called ....

A] Function Keys.

B] Numeric Keys.

C] Typewriter Keys.

D] Special purpose keys.

Q.21. The keyboard keys like Caps lock that turn on features on or off are called.

A] Function Keys.

B] Combination Keys.

C] Toggle Keys.

D] Special Purpose Keys.

Q.22. Word processing, electronic spread sheets, database managers and graphics programs are all grouped under the title.

A] Browsings Programs.

B] Operating System.

C] Application Software.

D] Data and Information.

Q.23. Keyboard, mouse, monitor, and system unit collectively also known as

A] Solid ware.

B] Software.

C] Hardware.

D] Firm ware.

Q.24. Output of an image on the monitor screen is often called soft copy.

A] True.

B] False.

Q.25. each 0 and 1 in the binary numbering system is called a bit.

A] True.

B] False.

Q.26. Catch memory is used to store most frequently accessed information from the RAM.

A] True.

B] False.

Q.27. The system board is also known as the main board or mother board.

A] True.

B] False.

Q.28. ASSCII, EBCDIC and Unicode are binary coding schemes.

A] True.

B] False.

Q.29. The keys labelled 0-9 on the keyboard are called.

A] Function Keys.

B] Numeric Keys.

C] Typewriter Keys.

D] Special purpose keys.

Q.30. A CD ROM stands for Compact Disk Read Only Memory.

A] True.

B] False.

Q.31. .... consists of step-by-step introductions that tells the computer how to complete the task.

A] Programs.

B] Hardware.

C] Data.

D] Objects.

Q.32. A CD-R stands for CD-Recordable.

A] True.

B] False.

Q.33.......... is a background soft ware that helps the computer to manage its internal resources.

A] System Software.

B] Information.

C] Objects.

D] None of these.

Q.34. Output of an image obtained using a printer is called as hard copy.

A] True.

B] False.

Q.35. Following are the file compression programs, EXCEPT

A] Win Zip.

B] RAID.

C] Win RAR.

D] PK Zip.

Q.36. A track on a disk is one of the many circular ring areas where data is written magnetically.

A] True.

B] False.

Q.37. Floppy disks are removable storage media.

A] True.

B] False.

Q.38. The keyboard keys that have arrows on them are called.

A] Function Keys.

B] Combination Keys.

C] Navigation Keys

D] Special Purpose Keys.

Q.39. Microprocessor is often called as CPU.

A] True.

B] False.

Q.40. Eight bits make up a bite.

A] True.

B] False.

Q.41. Output of an image on the monitor screen is often called hard copy.

A] True.

B] False.

Q.42.......... are graphical objects used to represent and open commonly used applications.

A] G.U.I..

B] Primers'.

C] Windows NT.

D] Icons.

Q.43. A CD-ROM means CD-RW.

A] True.

B] False.

Q.44. Data stored in RAM is

A] Is non-volatile.

B] Is only there while the power is on.

C] Remains only a few minutes after the power is turned off.

D] Is permanent and only lost in power failure.

Q.45. A CD-R stands for CD-Regional.

A] True.

B] False.

Q.46. Primary function of a monitor is to display information to the user.

A] True.

B] False.

Q.47. Random Access Memory] RAM. is .... type of memory.

A] Permanent.

B] Temporary.

C] Flash.

D] Smart.

Q.48 The external memory of the computer is present on the motherboard in the form of slots.

A] False.

B] True.

Q.49 The internal memory of the computer is present on the motherboard in the form of chips

A] True.

B] False.

Q.50 cache memory is used to store most frequently accessed information from the ram.

A] True.

B] False.

Q.1. The "System Date" and "System Time" are the date and time as maintained by the computer's internal clock.

A] True

B] False

Q.2. Disk cleanup is used to rearrange your files so that they are not broken up.

A] True

B] False

Q.3. In Window Vista a folder system is also called a "Directory System."

A] True

B] False

Q.4. "rtf" stands for "rich text format"

A] True

B] False

Q.5. You can click on.............. to learn how to use Windows Vista, obtain troubleshooting information, receive support and more.

A] "Search"

B] "Windows"

C] "Start"

D] "Help & Support"

Q.6. In MS paint to draw a curved line, we have to click the................... Icon.

A] "Curve"

B] "Line"

C] "Polygon"

D] "Rectangle"

Q.7. .... refers to the height and width of the characters to be printed.

A] "Font Size"

B] "Border"

C] "Cell"

D] "Font Style"

Q.8. There is button which is not present on the "Title bar".

A] Minimize

B] Start

C] Maximise

D] Close

Q.9. Disk Defragmenter is used to remove unnecessary files on your hard disk to free up space and your computer run faster.

A] True

B] False

Q.10. To change the size of your picture, Select "Image Attributes" from the menu.

A] True

B] False

Q.11. To start the calculator application click "Start" and select "All Programs Accessories Calculator."

A] True

B] False

Q.12. .... can be used to create and format large and complex text documents.

A] "Calculator"

B] "WordPad"

C] "Notepad"

D] "Text Pad"

Q.13. Notepad is a basic text editor that can be used to create simple documents.

A] True

B] False

Q.14. A folder system is also called a "................"

A] "Direction System"

B] "Directory System"

C] "Directory list"

D] "Folder book"

Q.15. A folder within a folder is known as a "Folder list."

A] True

B] False

Q.17. A .... is like a container in which you can store files.

A] "Icon"

B] "document"

C] "Folder"

D] "Sheet"

Q.18. The operating system's job is .... to

A] Execute many useful commands easily.

B] to make request for service through a defined application programme interface.

C] to control the computer at the most fundamental level.

D] None of these.

Q.19. The windows interface is based on ....

A] "Graphical user Interface" or GUI

B] Application Programme Interface or] API.

C] "Clipboard"

D] None of these

Q.20. The name of a file consists of two parts, the File Name and the sub file name.

A] True

B] False

Q.21. To access the location of the particular file quickly, you create a shortcut icon for the file and place it on the desktop.

A] True

B] False

Q.22. In Windows Vista windows sidebar contains mini-programs called gadgets.

A] True

B] False

Q.23. A file created using Notepad is stored with the extension.................
.

A] ".txt"

B] ".docx"

C] ".png"

D] ".jpg"

Q.24. In windows vista two types of "searchers" are supported: Regular search Instant search.

A] True

B] False

Q.25. When your computer is booted and is ready to use, the screen you see is called the ....

A] "Table top"

B] "Desktop"

C] "Laptop"

D] None of these

Q.26. "Computer" is an application which performs functions same as that of a handheld calculator.

A] True

B] False

Q.27. .... is designed to prevent and remove spy ware.

A] User Account Control

B] Windows Firewall

C] <u>Windows Defender</u>

D] Parental Controls

Q.28. The clipboard is not available in Windows Vista Programs.

A] True

B] <u>False</u>

Q.29. What is "Windows Aero"

A] It is the graphical user interface for Windows XP.

B] <u>It is the graphical user interface for Windows Vista.</u>

C] Application Program

D] None of these

Q.30. Which is the basic program of a computer?

A] <u>Operating System</u>

B] Software Program

C] Application Program

D] None of these

Q.31. As you type, the text automatically moves to the next line it reaches the right end of the margin. This feature is called "Word Wrap."

A] <u>True</u>

B] False

Q.32. "Log Off" is a power-saving state.

A] True

B] <u>False</u>

Q.33. In windows vista, you can see multiple programs running simultaneously on different areas of your screen.

A] <u>True</u>

B] False

Q.34. The .... Menu is used to enhance the appearance of the contained presented in a document.

A] "Insert"

B] "Edit" ?

C] <u>"Format"</u>

D] "File"

Q.35. The "text" tool is used to add text to a paint object.

A] <u>True</u>

B] False

Q.36. "............." helps in guarding your computer against malicious software.

A] "Windows Firewall"

B] "Windows Defender"

C] "Spy ware"

D] of these.

Q.37. .... is a basic text editing programme and it is most commonly used to view or edit text files.

A] "Calculator"

B] "Notepad"

C] "Address book"

D] "Paint"

Q.38. In a windows operating system screen saver

A] is helps in guarding your computer against many types of malicious software.

B] is a long, vertical bar that is displayed on the side of your desktop.

C] is a programme that displays on image, animation, or just a blank screen on a Computer after on input has been received for a certain length of time.

D] None of these.

Q.39. Features in Windows Vista make it easier, safer and more entertaining to use your PC virtually anytime and anywhere.

A] True

B] False

Q.40. The programmes on the .... in Windows Vista remain there and are always available for you to click to start them.

A] the "Most frequently use programmes list.

B] "pinned items list"

C] "Documents"

D] "Control Panel"

Q.41. In Windows Vista .... is a power-saving state.

A] Log off

B] Sleep

C] Restart

D] Lock

Q.42. AERO is an abbreviation of ....

A] Authentic, Energetic, Reflective and Open.

B] Essential, Reflective and Open.

C] Arithmetic, Essential, Reflective and Object.

D] Authentic, Essential, Reflective and Open.

Q.43. At the bottom of the screen, you can see a long, thin bar which is called as ....

A] "Task bar"

B] "Title bar"

C] "Menu bar"

D] "Spacebar"

Q.44. In Windows Vista a "Clipboard" is ....

A] an application program

B] a temporary storage area for information that you have copied or moved from one place and plan to use somewhere else.

C] an operating system.

D] None of these.

Q.45. .... is a basic text editing programme and it is most commonly used to view or edit text files.

A] "Calculator"

B] "Notepad"

C] "Address book"

D] "Paint"

Q.46. ...., is a drawing programme that can be used to create modify graphic images.

A] "Brush"

B] "Paint"

C] "Notepad"

D] "WordPad"

Q.47. The .... menu is used to enhance the apperance of the content presented in a document.

A] "Insert"

B] "Edit"

C] "Format"

D] "File"

Q.48. A .... is a rectangular section on the screen that is used to display information and other programme.

A] Icon

B] Desktop

C] Window

D] Panel

Q.49. The capability of an operating system to run multiple programmes at the same time is called "Multitasking."

A] <u>True</u>

B] False

Q.50. In Window vista, you can see multiple Programme running simultaneously on different areas of your screen

A]<u>True</u>

B] False

Q.51. The name of a file consist of two parts

A] Folder Name

B] use Extension

C] <u>File Name</u>

D] use Sub folder Name

Q.52. We can navigate through text using

A] Cpu

B] <u>Mouse</u>

C] Key board

D] Monitor

Q.1. In MS Word 2007 when text is selected, a "..........." is automatically displayed.

A] Taskbar

B] Main Toolbar

C] <u>Mini Toolbar</u>

D] Menu bar

Q.2. You can make for a TOC using:

A] Heading styles.

B] Custom styles.

C] Outline levels.

D] <u>All of these.</u>

Q.3. .... contains command for opening, saving, printing and closing a file.

A] "Home"

B] <u>"Office Button"</u>

C] "View"

D] "Insert"

Q.4. .... offers a wide variety of options to design documents.

A] Microsoft Excel

B] Microsoft PowerPoint

C] <u>Microsoft Word</u>

D] Microsoft Access

Q.5. All of the following Ribbon tabs are displayed in Word 2007, EXCEPT

A] Home

B] Insert

C] Tools

D] Page Layout

Q.6. When you use the mouse to move the insertion point, the shape of mouse pointer is like I-beam.

A] True

B] False

Q.7. Index shows you at a glance, the topics that are included in the document and make it easier to locate information.

A] True

B] False

Q.8. You can click on the "Format" tab under "WordArt tools" to modify the WordArt as per your requirements.

A] True

B] False

Q.9. In Word, a file is called as a ....

A] "template"

B] "form"

C] "database"

D] "Document"

Q.10. The Mail Marge feature, combines a list of data, typically a file of names and addresses.

A]True

B] False

Q.11. Microsoft Word is the only word processor available in the market.

A] True

B] False

Q.12. Hyperlink identifies a location in the document or a section of text that you name for feature reference.

A] True

B] False

Q.13. A .... is a reference from one part of a document to related information in same another part.

A] Hyperlink

B] Cross-reference

C] Document

D] Linkage

Q.14. For Indentation you may use the "Decrease Indent" and "Increase Indent" icons in the "Paragraph" group on the "............" tab for indenting your text.

A] Insert

B] <u>Home</u>

C] Page Layout

D] Data

Q.15. In MS Word 2007 the "References" tab contains spell check, the squares, and track changes.

A] True

A] <u>False</u>

Q.16. The "..............." is a dictionary of synonyms which you can use to find words that are synonyms with a term.

A] Translate

B] Spelling

<u>C] Thesaurus</u>

D] Research

Q.17. A " .... " is a listing of the topics that appear in a document with their associated page references.

A] Index

B] Table

C] Clipboard

D] <u>Table of contents</u>

Q.18. You can format your document automatically applying styles, available in MS Word 2007.

A] <u>True</u>

B] False

Q.19. A "............." is a connection to a location in the current document to another document or Web Site.

A] Link

B] <u>hyperlink</u>

C] hypolink

D] linkage

Q.20. To view a document in the Print Preview Mode, click on the Office Button and select "Print Print Preview."

A] <u>True</u>

B] False

Q.21. You may use the "The Auto Complete Feature" to automatically correct the grammatical and spelling mistakes in your document.

A] True

B] False

Q.22. Using a word Processing application you can create, modify, store, retrieve and print a document.

A] True

B] False

Q.23. "Mini Toolbar" provides easy way to access the most frequently used formatting commands.

A] True

B] False

Q.24. To print only selected pages in your documnet, you may use either the "Current page" or "Page" option under "Print Range."

A] True

B] False

Q.25. MS Word 2007 when we click on the Office Button the "Edit" menu is displayed.

A] True

B] False

Q.26. A "................" is a pre-designed document useful for creating common purpose documents such as a fax, invoice or business letter.

A] Template

B] File

C] Form

D] Database

Q.27. A multileve list shows the list items at different levels rather then single level.

A] True

B] False

Q.28. A "............" is used to organize information into an easy-to-read format of horizontal rows and vertical columns.

A] Cell

B] Sheet

C] Box

D] Table

Q.29. To remove individual character at the left you may press "............".

A] Delete

B] Backspace

C] Enter

D] Spacebar

Q.30. When you click on "Format Printer" icon on the "Home" tab, you can see that your mouse pointer changes to a "............" icon.

A] paintbrush

B] I-beam

C] Arrow

D] 4-Way arrow

Q.31. You may create a new document using standard templates provided by Word by checking on a template name in the "New Document" window.

A] True

B] False

Q.32. MS Word's Mail Merge feature facilitates you to mail your document about special offers to a large number of people.

A] True

B] False

Q.33. When you move your mouse over a button, a .... is displayed. That provides a detailed description of what the button does.

A] Super-tooltip

B] Sub-tooltip

C] Info

D] Key-tip

Q.34. MS Word 2007 can quickly sort text, data or numbers ascending or descending order.

A] True

B] False

Q.35. .... Applications help you to create different types of written documents such as personal letters, from letters, brochures, faxes and even professional manuals.

A] Word Processor

B] Word Pad

C] Note Pad

D] None of these

Q.36. The "Mailings" tab contains the items required for mail merge.

A] True

B] False

Q.37. Word places footnotes at the end of each page and end notes at the end of documents.

A] True

B] False

Q.38. To remove the hyperlink while retaining the text, right - click on it and select "Remove Hyperlink."

A] True

B] False

Q.39. MS Word indicates formatting inconsistencies with a red wavy underline.

A] True

B] False

Q.40. To automatically correct the document, we use

A] The auto correct feature

B] The auto complete feature

C] Formatting

D] Building Blocks

Q.41. A "..............." is a common application for news paper columns.

A] News reading

B] News letter

C] News

D] News editor

Q.42. Personal letters, form letters, brochures, faxes and professional manuals can be using word processors.

A] True

B] False

Q.43. The set margins, select "Margins" from the "Page Setup" group on the "Page Layout" tab.

A] True

B] False

Q.44. Drop caps are the first characters at the beginning of a paragraph that are enlarged, conversing several lines.

A] True

B] False

Q.45. A multilevel list shows the list items at different levels rather than single level.

A] True

B] False

Q.46. The "Page Layout" tab contains margin, orientation, and spacing properties.

A] True

B] False

Q.47. A "............" is used to mark a certain location in a document.

A] Index

B] Hyperlink

C] Bookmark

D] Table

Q.48. You may click on "Replace All" button to replace all occurrences of the search text by specified new text.

A] True

B] False

Q.49. While working on a document in MS Word 2007 when we click on the picture, it is surrounded by eight boxes called "Sizing handles" which is used to to change the size of the graphic.

A] True

B] False

Q.50. While changing the level of an item in hierarchy you can increase the indent by using

A] "Tab"

B] "Backspace"

C] "Delete"

D] "Spacebar"

Q.51. Footnotes or Endnotes are used to provide certain "........................".

A] References

B] Information

C] Points

D] Lists

Q.52. If you want the data to be automatically get updated in a document when the current data changes, check the "Update automatically" box.

A] True

B] False

Q.1. In formula bar, an adjacent range is specified by giving the starting and editing cell addresses separated by a

A] Semicolon

B] Comma

C] Full stop

D] Colon

Q.2. The cell address is displayed in the "Text Box".

A] True

B] False

Q.3. A .... is a visual representation of data and conveys the information in an easy to understand and attractive manner.

A] chart

B] table

C] picture

D] graphic

Q.4. In formulas, a non-adjacent range is specified by giving the cell addresses separated by a ....

A] Semicolon

B] Comma

C] Full stop

D] Colon

Q.5. You can use the .... to enter and edit data, instead of editing directly in your work sheet.

A] formula bar

B] title bar

C] menu bar

D] space bar

Q.6. Your Excel 2007 file is stored with the extension "............".

A] ".docx"

B] ".xlsx"

C] ".xltx"

D] ".zltx"

Q.7. In an electronic spreadsheet or worksheet, data can be edited, new data can be added, and unwnated data can be deleted.

A] True

B] False

Q.8. The "Review" tab contains proofing tools like spell check & also has button that let you add comments to a worksheet and manage revisions.

A] True

B] False

Q.9. The "............" tab contains proofing tools like spell check.

A] "Review"

B] "Data"

C] "View"

D] "Insert"

Q.10. You can create and design our own work book templates.

A] True

B] False

Q.11. In a spreadsheet programme as you move from one cell to another, the reference or address to the active cell appears in the "Name Box."

A] True

B] False

Q.12. To start the Microsoft Excel Application, click on the "Start" button and select "All programmes Microsoft Office ? Microsoft Office Excel 2007.

A] True

B] False

Q.13. The "Insert" tab lets you add special ingredients like tables, graphics, charts, and hyperlinks in a spreadsheets programme.

A] True

B] False

Q.14. The text that appears in the bottom margin of the page is called as the "Footer".

A] True

B] False

Q.15. In Excel, a formula always begins with an equal sign] =. and uses arithmetic operators like +, -, *, /, %, and ^ to perform addition, subtraction, multiplication, division, percent and exponentiation respectively.

A] True

B] False

Q.16. While working you may have to reference data from more than one sheet which is called referencing multiple sheets.

A] True

B] False

Q.17. The defalut page orientation setting is "Landscape".

A] True

B] False

Q.18. "............." is a method which aids you in forecasting values.

A] "Find"

B] "Replace"

C] "Goal Seek"

D] "Go to"

Q.19. In MS Excel 2007, below the "Ribbon", we can see Name Box on the left and the Formula Bar on the right.

A] <u>True</u>

B] False

Q.20. A "..............." is a prewritten formula the performs calculations automatically.

A] <u>"Function"</u>

B] "Equation"

C] "Template"

D] "Reaction"

Q.21. MS Excel 2007 is used for different types of .... varying from vary simple to complex.

A] <u>calculations</u>

B] manipulations

C] presentations

D] expressions

Q.22. Your excel file is stored with the extension ".xltx".

A] True

B] <u>False</u>

Q.23. "Autocorrect" is a feature of Microsoft Excel 2007 that makes entering a series of heading easier by logically repeating and extending the series.

A] True

B] <u>False</u>

Q.24. "A relative reference" is a cell or range reference used in a formula whose location does not change when a formula is copied.

A] True

B] <u>False</u>

Q.25. While changing the level of an item in the hierarchy you can increase the indent by using.

A] <u>"Tab"</u>

B] "Backspace"

C] "Delete"

D] "Spacebar"

Q.26. To set margins, select "Margins" from the "Page Setup" group on the "Page Layout" tab.

A] <u>True</u>

B] False

Q.27. To remove individual character at the left you may press "..............".

A] Delete

B] Backspace

C] Enter

D] Spacebar

Q.28. Drop caps are the first character/s at the beginning that are enlarged, conversing several lines.

A] True

B] False

Q.29. The intersection of a row and a column is called a "................".

A] Table

B] Cell

C] Data

D] Sheet

Q.30. A .... is a file that is provided by the application in a "ready to use" format.

A] Sheet

B] Template

C] Book

D] Report

Q.31. A .... is a visual representation of data and conveys the information in a easy to understand and attractive manner.

A] Chart

B] Table

C] Picture

D] Graphic

Q.32. To move among the worksheet in your workbook, you need to click on the "Workbook" tab.

A] True

B] False

Q.33. A theme comprise of a colour palette, font set, and effects.

A] True

B] False

Q.34. You can view two areas of worksheet and lock rows or columns in one area by splitting or freezing panes.

A] True

B] False

Q.35. "............" are individual designs that can be applied to different parts to the document.

A] "Graphics"

B] "Styles"

C] "Pictures"

D] "Themes"

Q.36. "............" contains commands for opening, saving, printing, and closing a file.

A] "View" tab

B] "Office Button"

C] "Insert" tab

D] "Review" tab

Q.37. When a formula containing an absolute cell reference is copied to another row or column in the worksheet, the cell reference does not change.

A] True

B] False

Q.38. The "header" is usually the title you give on the page.

A] True

B] False

Q.39. The text that appears in the top margin of the page is called the ....

A] Footer

B] Column

C] Header

D] Paragraph

Q.40. In a spreadsheet programme a table is a selection of two or more cells.

A] True

B] False

Q.41. The "title" is usually given as the footer.

A] True

B] False

Q.42. To stop the automatic relative cell references, i.e. to make the cell reference absolute, type a .... character before the column and row number.

A] # hash.

B] $ dollar.

C] % percent.

D] * star.

Q.43. A theme comprise of a colour palette, font set, and effects.

A] True

B] False

Q.44. To select a group or range of cells, click on the cell you want to begin, drag your cursor and release it when you have reached the end of the selection.

A] True

B] False

Q.45. If we require to add more data to be on one page, we change the page orientation to land scape.

A] True

B] False

Q.46. Each worksheet can be used to organized different types of related information.

A] True

B] False

Q.47. The "table" is a visual representation of data and convey the information in an easy to understand and attractive manner.

A] True

B] False

Q.48. "Themes" provided with MS Excel 2007 are universal designs that unify all of the styles.

A] True

B] False

Q.49. In Microsoft Excel 2007, a single file or document is called a ".............".

A] Workbook

B] Worksheet

C] Sheet

D] Notebook

Q.50. "Notebook" contains a collection of one or more worksheets and, optionally, chart sheets containing graphic pictures of your worksheet data.

A] True

B] False

Q.51. With the .... option, you can freeze either or both, rows and columns ie. regardless of where you are in the worksheet you can see the information in these rows and/or columns at all times.

A] Split
B] Arrange
C] Fitter
D] Freeze Panes

Q.52. You can create charts to represent data more effectively in an electronic sheet or worksheet.

A] True
B] False

Q.53. In a spreadsheet each cell has its own address called as "cell address".

A] True
B] False

Q.54. A template file in MS Excel 2007 has an extension "................".

A] .docx
B] .yltx
C] .xltx
D] .zltx

Q.55. A "............" is like an accountant's ledger consisting of rows and columns.

A] Table
B] Microsoft Excel 2007
C] Format
D] Sheet

Q.56. A "table" is a visual representation of data and conveys the information in an easy to understand and attractive manner.

A] True
B] False

Q.1. The "Insert" tab contains the basic set of objects which you can insert into a slide.

A] True
B] False

Q.2. Click "Replace All" to replace all occurrences of search text by the specified new text.

A] True
B] False

Q.3. A "................" graphic is a visual representation of your information and ideas.

A] "WordArt"

B] "ClipArt"

C] "SmartArt"

D] "Autoshape"

Q.4. To start a Microsoft PowerPoint Application, click on the "Start" button and select "All progrmmes ? Microsoft Office ? Microsoft Office PowerPoint 2007".

A] True

B] False

Q.5. "..............." refer to a ready-to-use picture.

A] "WordArt"

B] "ClipArt"

C] "SmartArt"

D] "Autoshape"

Q.6. To open a recently used presentation you may click the office button and then click on the presentation name in the list displayed under "Recent Documents".

A] True

B] False

Q.7. SmartArt programs are designed to help you to create an effective presentation.

A] True

B] False

Q.8. The "............." tab contains tools that controls how to slide show is presented.

A] "Design"

B] "Slide Show"

C] "Review"

D] "View"

Q.9. Minature pictures of slides displayed in the slide sorter view.

A] True

B] False

Q.10. .... which displays icon that represent commonly used commands such as Save, Undo, and Redo.

A] Home Button

B] The Ribbon

C] The Quick Access Tool bar

D] The Office Button

Q.11. A "..........." is a connection to a location in the current documnet, another document or a website.

A] Highlink

B] hipolink

C] linkage

D] hyperlink

Q.12. .... are used to create slide shows on the computer

A] Presentation graphics

B] Analytical development programs

C] Super Slide packages

D] Slide maker tools

Q.13. To preview your presentation as web page, you need to add the "Web Page Preview" command to Ribbon.

A] True

B] False

Q.14. With "Slide Show View" you can see how your graphics timings, movies, animated elements and transition effects will look in the actulashow.

A] True

B] False

Q.15. In graphic presentation, programmes each presentation is divided into ....

A] charts

B] slides

C] tables

D] pictures

Q.16. In PowerPoint "Match case": you may check this box for a case sensitive search.

A] True

B] False

Q.17. "Scale to fit paper": check this box to print the slides with an outer frame.

A] True

B] False

Q.18. In PowerPoint "build effects" are animations to slide contents..

A] True

B] False

Q.19. A "..............." is a pre-designed presentation designed for common purpose such as photo album or a quiz show.

A] "Chart"

B] "Table"

C] "Slide"

D] <u>"Template"</u>

Q.20. You may create a new presentation using a template provided by PowerPoint.

A] <u>True</u>

B] False

Q.21. We can insert a video clip on a PowerPoint Slide.

A] <u>True</u>

B] False

Q.22. When you move your mouse over a sizing handle the pointer becomes a ".............".

A] Round Arrow

B] <u>Two-headed Arrow</u>

C] Plus Sign

D] Four-headed Arrow

Q.23. PowerPoint Presentation is a component of following application software.

A] Leap Office

B] Start Office

C] Open Office

D] <u>MS Office</u>

Q.24. "Slide Show View" is an exclusive view of your slides in thumbnail form.

A] True

B] <u>False</u>

Q.25. Headers and Footers are used to add information such as slide numbers, the time and date, a company logo or the presentation title to the top of a hand out or notes page in your presentation, or to bottom of a slide, handout or notes page.

A] <u>True</u>

B] False

Q.26. To see a preview of your slide in a window on the screen, click on the Quick Access Toolbar and select "Print ? Print Preview".

A] True

B] False

Q.27. In Graphics Presentation Programs each presentation is divided into charts.

A] True

B] False

Q.28. Using WordArt graphics, you can effectively communicate your message in a quick and msimple way.

A] True

B] False

Q.29. You may change the presentation views by checking on the buttons displayed on the "..........." at the bottom of the screen.

A] "Title bar"

B] "Menu bar"

C] "Tool bar"

D] "Status bar"

Q.30. "Animations" refers to addition of special visual or sound effect to your slides.

A] True

B] False

Q.31. Using PowerPoint presentation graphics is simple and it is used for effective presentation

A] on a topic.

B] True

C] False

Q.32. A "review" is a way to looking at a presentation.

A] True

B] False

Q.33. In Presentation Graphics "..........." are used to add information such as slide numbers, the time and date, a company logo or the presentation title to the top of a handout or notes page in your presentation, or a bottom of a slide, handout or notes.

A] Hyperlinks

B] Tables

C] Header and Footers

D] Charts

Q.34. The sizing handles at the slides are used to adjust only the height or the width.

A] True

B] False

Q.35. "..............." takes up the full computer screen, like an actual slide show presentation.

A] Slide Sorter View

B] Normal View

C] Slide Show View

D] Notes Page

Q.36. The "Outline" tab shows your slide text in outline form.

A] True

B] False

Q.37. A slide layout refers to the arrangements of elements, such as text, pictures, tables, charts and movies, on a slide.

A] True

B] False

Q.38. If you have a large number of slides in your presentation, you may find it more convenient to use the .... to view all your slides and change their positions.

A] Normal View

B] Slide Sorter View

C] Slide Show View

D] Notes Page

Q.39. You may use either the Normal View or the Slide Sorter View to delete a Slide.

A] True

B] False

Q.40. In Microsoft PowerPoint your file is stored with the .... extension.

A] psd

B] .rtf

C] .pptx

D] .docx

Q.41. When the pointer becomes a ...., you can drag placeholder to the location you wish.

A] Round arrow

B] Two-round arrow

C] Plus sign

D] Four-headed arrow

Q.42. A "Clip" may be a single media file, including art, sound, animation or movies.

A] True

B] False

Q.43. "..........." are details about a file that help identify it.

A] Desktop Properties

B] Window Properties

C] Advanced Properties

D] Document Properties

Q.44. The "Sizing Handles" at the slides and corners of the selection rectangle can be used to adjust the size of the place holder.

A] True

B] False

Q.45. To open a file that you have previously saved, click the Ribbon and select "Open".

A] True

B] False

Q.46. "............." is the main editing view.

A] Slide Sorter View

B] Normal View

C] Slide Show View

D] Notes Page

Q.47. We can insert a audio clip on a powerpoint slide.

A] True

B] False

Q.48. In PowerPoint the "Insert" tab contains tools to design your slides.

A] True

B] False

Q.49. The "..........." tab contains the basic formatting tools.

A] "Design"

B] "View"

C] "Insert"

D] "Home"

Q.50. The "Slides" tab makes it easy to navigate through your presentation and to see the effects of changes and also rearrange, add or delete sliders.

A] True

B] False

Q.51. The "Outline" tab shows you slides as your thumbnail sized images while you edit.

A] True

B] False

Q.52. In PowerPoint the "Insert" tab contains tools to design your slides.

A] True

B] False

Q.1. You can start the name of the field with a space.

A] True.

B] False.

Q.2. "............" is a database object that is mainly used to enter and display records and make changes to existing records on screens.

A] query.

B] form.

C] report.

D] table.

Q.3. Primary Number is a unique, sequential number that is automatically incremented by one whenever a new record is added to the table.

A] True.

B] False.

Q.4. each column is a record which is the smallest unit of information about a record.

A] True.

B] False.

Q.5. A form is a printed output generated from tables and queries.

A] True.

B] False.

Q.6. The ribbon has Task-oriented Tabs, Groups and command buttons.

A] True.

B] False.

Q.7. "............" is an electronic database management system which can store, organize access, manipulate, and present information in many different ways.

A] MS Access 2007.

B] MS Word.

C] MS Excel.

D] MS PowerPoint.

Q.8. A professional database is the most widely used database structure.

A] True.

B] False.

Q.9. The tables are related or linked to one another by a common field.

A] True.

B] False.

Q.10. When you select a data type, its default properties are displayed under "Display Properties."

A] True.

B] False.

Q.11. "............" data type is used to store numbers only.

A] Auto Number.

B] Text.

C] Number.

D] Date/Time.

Q.12. A default value is used to specify a value that is automatically entered in a field when a new record is added.

A] True.

B] False.

Q.13. "............" stores the information in Access 2007.

A] Table.

B] Queries.

C] Reports.

D] Forms.

Q.14. A field property is a characteristic that helps to define a field.

A] True.

B] False.

Q.15. ".........." data type is used to store images, documents, graphs etc.

A] Hyperlink.

B] OEL Object.

C] Text.

D] Description.

Q.16. ".........." decides the maximum number of characters that can be entered in the field.

A] Format.

B] Input Mask.

C] Caption.

D] Field Size.

Q.17. The information in a database is stored in a ....

A] Chart.

B] Box.

C] Folder.

D] Table.

Q.18. "............" is the default data type and is used to store text entries like words, combinations of words and numbers and numbers that are not used in calculations.

A] Text.

B] Number.

C] Memo.

D] Currency.

Q.19. In Access, you can sort data in ascending or descending order.

A] True.

B] False.

Q.20. Access provides different window formats called "Lists" to display and work with the objects in a database.

A] True.

B] False.

Q.21. In Access, every database is stored in a single file which has the extension.

A] ".docx"

B] ".rtf"

C] ".accdb"

D] ".txt"

Q.22. The data type defines the type of data the field will contain.

A] True.

B] False.

Q.23. A .... is used to identify the data stored in a field.

A] Table.

B] Field Name.

C] Box.

D] Bracket.

Q.24. A database is an organized collection of related information.

A] True.

B] False.

Q.25. ".........." simplifies data entry and controls what data is required and how it is to be displayed.

A] Format.

B] Input Mask.

C] Caption.

D] Field Size.

Q.26. Access automatically creates a code for the primary key, which helps makes queries and other operations.

A] True.

B] False.

Q.27. .... provides a number of data types.

A] Word 2007.

B] Access 2007.

C] Excel 2007.

D] PowerPoint 2007.

Q.28. It is difficult to add, delete and modify records from a table.

A] True.

B] False.

Q.29. The "Form Wizard" feature of Access 2007 makes it very easy to design forms.

A] True.

B] False.

Q.30. When you open a database or create a new one, the names of your database objects such a tables. Forms and reports appear in the Navigation Pane.

A] True.

B] False.

Q.31. Charts are made up of vertical columns] called fields. and horizontal rows] called records.

A] True.

B] False.

Q.32. You can quickly produce reports using some MS Access features.

A] True.

B] False.

Q.33."..........." are windows that you create and arrange in order to easily view or change the information in a table.

A] Table.

B] Queries.

C] Report.

D] Forms.

Q.34. "………." restricts the data easy to meet certain conditions or requirements.

A] Validation Text.

B] Default Value.

C] Validation Rule.

D] Format.

Q.35. Forms help you print same or all of the information in a table.

A] True.

B] False.

Q.36. "……….." data type is used to store text that is too long to be stored in a text field.

A] Text.

B] Number.

C] Memo.

D] Currency.

Q.37. The "Description" text box is used to describe the field.

A] True.

B] False.

Q.38. "…………" specifies a field caption or a prompt for the user to enter data.

A] Format.

B] Input Mask.

C] Caption.

D] Field Size.

Q.39. "Form Wizard" guides you through the steps required to create a form.

A] True.

B] False.

Q.40. A field name is to identify the data stored in a field.

A] True.

B] False.

Q.41. A default value is an expression that defines acceptable values.

A] True.

B] False.

Q.42. Each row is a field which contains all the information about a person, thing or place.

A] True.

B] False.

Q.43. A primary key must be

A] Unique But Permit Null.

B] Unique and Not Null.

C] Non-unique And Not Null.

D] Non-unique And Permit Null.

Q.44. which of the following are functions performed by a DBA?

A] Database Design.

B] System Security.

C] Backup and Recovery.

D] All of the above.

Q.45. "..........." is a relation database management application that is used to create and analyze a database.

A] Word 2007.

B] Access 2007.

C] System Security.

D] PowerPoint 2007.

Q.46. You can create as many tables as you need to store different types of information.

A] True.

B] False.

Q.47. A "............" is a field or set of fields in your table that provide Access with a unique identifier for every record.

A] Password.

B] Special Code.

C] Primary Key.

D] Unique Code.

Q.48. The photo can be inserted as a file.

A] True.

B] False.

Q.49. You can analyze the data in a table and perform calculations on different fields of data.

A] True.

B] False.

Q.50. Formatting the data often helps in finding some particular information quickly.

A] True.

B] False.

Q.51. what is the first step of defining a database.

A] Designing the database.

B] Collection of data.

C] Planning your database.

D] Digitizing your data.

Q.52. The "Print Preview" tab appears when you view the table in the print preview mode.

A] True.

B] False.

Q.53. Datasheet view can be used to create and view the design of all types of database objects such as tables, forms, queries, and reports.

A] True.

B] False.

Q.54. DBMS means..................

A] Database Management System.

B] Domain Management System.

C] Domain Manangeemt Server.

D] Domain Management Style.

Q.55. Access also ensure that every record has a non-blank primary key field, and that it is always unique.

A] True.

B] False.

Q.56. “Validation Rule” specifies a default value for a field to be automatically field n at the time of data entry.

A] True.

B] False.

Q.57. Design view provides a row and column view of the data in tables, forms, and queries.

A] True.

B] False.

Q.58 You can enter up to charactess in a text field.

A] 375

B] 125

C] 235

D] 255

Q.1. Netscape Navigator is a type of ....

A] Utility Program.

B] Operating System.

C] Browser.

D] Web Authoring Program.

Q.2. When you type an address such as "http://www.mkcl.org", in this .org indicates.

A] Original Web Site.

B] Commercial Web Site.

C] Organizational Web Site.

D] Educational Web Site.

Q.3. You can search the World Wide Web for a specific topic by using .... and.................

A] Gophers, Fido's.

B] Scanner, Search Engine.

C] Search Engines, Indexes.

D Browsers, Larkers.

Q.4. A] n. .... is a set of rules for how information and messages are sent over the internet.

A] Protocol.

B] ISP.

C] Applet.

D] HTML Hyper Text Markup Language.

Q.5. Discussion on the internet about specific topic is known as

A] News.

B] News group.

C] Veronica.

D] Telnet.

Q.6. Which of the following is not a type of protocol?

A] TCI/IP

B] ASCII

C] None of these.

D] ppp

Q.7. Which of the following is a type of protocol?

A] ASCII

B] RAM

C] TCI/IP

D] DBA

Q.8. The three parts of an e-mail message are

A] TCP/IP, Domain and ISP.

B] Destination, Device and Sender.

C] Header, Message and Signature.

D] TCP, IP and Message.

Q.9. The network connecting several computers all over the world is?

A] Intranet.

B] Internet.

C] Arpanet.

D] Network.

Q.10. Which of the following is a browser.

A] Web site.

B] Microsoft.

C] Internet Explorer.

D] www.

Q.11. The terms DNS stands for.

A] Data Naming System.

B] Do Name System.

C] Domain Name System.

D] Duplicate Name System.

Q.12. Internet e-mail address is .... for every user.

A] Unique.

B] Same.

C] Common.

D] None of these.

Q.13. For navigating any website, user has to enter

A] URL.

B] www.

C] PPP.

D] None of these.

Q.14. What is the full form of E-Commerce ?

A] English Commerce.

B] Electronic Commerce.

C] Electric Commerce.

D] Element Commerce.

Q.15. To send e-mail to someone you need ....

A] Resident Address.

B] Internet Connectivity.

C] Fax Address.

D] None of these.

Q.16. .... is used to see the web page.

A] Inbox.

B] Recycle bin.

C] Internet Explorer.

D] Network Neighbourhood.

Q.17. Full form of URL

A] Universal Resource Locator.

B] Uniform Resource Locator.

C] Uni Resource Locator.

D] None of these.

Q.18. Modem converts data from a CD to a hard disk.

A] True.

B] False.

Q.19. Which of the following is a search engine.

A] Google.

B] Alta Vista.

C] Yahoo.

D] All of these.

Q.20. What is meant by E-Commerce?

A] Online selling, purchasing, account handling etc.

B] Subject commerce stream.

C] Electronic equipment to deal with commercial problem.

D] All of the above.

Q.21. . The extensions .gov, .edu, .mil, and .net are called.

A] DNSs.

B] E-mail targets.

C] Domain codes.

D] Mail to address.

Q.22. Web spiders and crawlers are examples of

A] Browsers.

B] Search Engines.

C] HTML Programs.

D] Flames.

Q.23. What is an URL ?

A] A software package used to cruise the World Wide Web..

B] The address of a resource on the World Wide Web.

C] The terms used to describe an internal wizard.

D] A live chat program [Unlimited real time language.

Q.24. What does the abbreviation "www." stands for.

A] World Wide Web.

B] Wide Wide Web.

C] World Width Web.

D] World with Web.

Q.25. Website that allows the user to search for data on keywords is:

A] Chat engines.

B] Routers.

C] Web Server.

D] Search engines.

Q.26. Which of the following web search engine is used worldwide?

A] Domain.

B] Google.

C] Toggle.

D] None of these.

Q.27. When you use a(n) .... to search for a topic, the information you search through is organized into a database like structure.

A] Search engine.

B] Index.

C] Spider.

D] Applet.

Q.28. Which of the following system electronic letter or message sent between individuals or computers.

A] E-mail.

B] Online Service.

C] Share Resources.

D] Voice mail messaging.

Q.29. To add current web to the favourites list.

A] Click "Favourites - Add to Favourites".

B] Click "Add - Favourites.

C] Click "File - Favourites.

D] All of these.

Q.30. Moving around the web from one site to another is referred to as................

A] Linking.

B] Navigating.

C] Hopping.

D] Paging.

Q.31. A protocol defines the rules for passing information between two or more computers.

A] True.

B] False.

Q.32. Information sent over the Internet is divided into small pieces called.

A] Packets.

B] PPPs.

C] e-mail forms.

D] Messages.

Q.33. Protocols like PPP and SLIP are used for.

A] Data Transfer.

B] Dialup internet connection.

C] Domain Registration.

D] None of these.

Q.34. The .com indicates websites of............. Types of organization.

A] Commercial.

B] Complex.

C] Company.

D] Cargo.

Q.35. Sending messages on the internet to another person's mailbox is

A] E-Business.

B] E-Letter.

C] E-Mail.

D] Cyber Mali.

Q.1. This is a type of personal information managers.

A] MS Word 2007

B] MS Excel 2007

C] MS PowerPoint 2007

D] MS Outlook 2007

Q.2. You can attach all sorts of files to an e-mail including Spreadsheets, word processor document database, even sound recordings and graphic images.

A] True

B] False

Q.3. To create a mail, We click on "Mail in the navigation pane.

A] True

B] False

Q.4. You uses the "Send/Receive" button to Send and receive mails.

A] True.

B] False.

Q.5. If you want to personalize your work environments wish to use a tool that organizes your contacts. Schedules etc. You will use.

A] Microsoft Office Excel 2007

B] Microsoft Office PowerPoint 2007

C] <u>Microsoft Office Outlook 2007</u>

D] Microsoft Office Word 2007

Q.6. Entry in MS Outlook 2007, that losts for more than 24 hours is called as

A] <u>Event</u>

B] Exhibition

C] Mail

D] Calendar

Q.7. Creating a Mail massage is also known as "Consolidating" a mail.

A] True.

B] <u>False.</u>

Q.8. The most important feature of outlook 2007 is sending and receiving an e-mail.

A] <u>True.</u>

B] False.

Q.9. A .... is a descriptive keyboard or phrase used in MS Outlook 2007 in which you can assign related items.

A] <u>Category</u>

B] Mail

C] Notes

D] Point

Q.10. Sourting tasks are the process of rearranging items in ascending order.

A] <u>True.</u>

B] False.

Q.11. The "Notebook" is an electronic book. which includes detailed information of all the people with whom you communicate.

A] True.

B] <u>False.</u>

Q.12. .... are separate external files that are along with you e-mail message.

A] <u>Attachments</u>

B] Options

C] E-mails

D] Parcels

Q.13. A task is a personal work related action item.

A] True.

B] False.

Q.14. The "Instant Search" Feature helps you to quickly find items in Microsoft Office Outlook 2007.

A] True.

B] False.

Q.15. In MS Outlook 2007 you can update the status of the tasks at any time and specify and percentage completed.

A] True.

B] False.

Q.16. If you add a recipient's name using "BCC" the name is not Visible to other recipients of the message.

A] True.

B] False.

Q.17. When you start Microsoft Outlook 2007. All the mails that you receive gets deposited in your "Inbox" Folder as default.

A] True.

B] False.

Q.18. Once We click on the flag symbol next to an important mail it gets added in the To Do Bar.

A] True.

B] False.

Q.19. You may need to save your contacts to a file, so that are available for use in the future. This is called................

A] "Saving"

B] "Importing"

C] "Exporting"

D] "Extracting"

Q.20. A Mailing list is a collection of contacts.

A] True.

B] False.

Q.21. To Forward that mail that you have received, click on the mail from the inbox and then click the "Forward" button.

A] True.

B] False.

Q.22. "Notes" are an electronic version of paper notes that you use to go down quick reminders.

A] True

B] False

Q.23. If you add a recipient's name using "Cc", the name is not visible to other recipients of the message.

A] True.

B] False.

Q.24. When you open Microsoft Outlook 2007, you will see a navigation pane on the left. Which contains catefories such as mail, calender and contacts etc?

A] True.

B] False.

Q.25. In the Tasks Timeline view in MS Outlook 2007. The tasks are arranged according to their due dates.

A] True.

B] False.

Q.26. Sorting "Categories" is the process of rearranging items in ascending or descending order.

A] True.

B] False.

Q.27. In MS Outlook 2007 you may add contacts form different books into your mailing list.

A] True.

B] False.

Q.28. When you went to convey the information that you have received to your friend or any other person you may .... the mail that you have received.

A] "Share"

B] "Give"

C] "Send"

D] "Forward"

Q.29. "Cc" stands for carbon copy and "Bcc" stands for blind carbon copy.

A] True.

B] False.

Q.30. The .... is an electronic book, which includes detailed information of all the people with whom you communicate.

A] Address book

B] Calendar

C] Task

D] Notebook

Q.31. You can use a flag to quickly create a follow-up item that can be tracked in the To-Do-Bar, in your Inbox, and even in he calendar.

A] True.

B] False.

Q.32. You can sort your tasks in MS Outlook 2007 according to subject by selecting "View Arrange By Subject".

A] True.

B] False.

Q.33. When you start Microsoft Outlook 2007, all the mails that you receive get deposited in your "Drafts" folder as default.

A] True.

B] False.

Q.1. When a web site is developed; the various interlinked files are grouped together. This is achieved using which facility.

A] Hypertext.

B] Hyperlinks.

C] Network.

D] None of these.

Q.2. What does the abbreviation "www" in internet stands for:

A] World Wide Web.

B] Wide Wide Web.

C] World Width Web.

D] World with Web.

Q.3. .... is one of the fastest growing internet applications.

A] E-mail.

B] Shopping.

C] Investing.

D] Commerce.

Q.4. .... is the new computer language used to write animation and games for the World Wide Web.

A] Java.

B] C.

C] C++.

D] HTML.

Q.5. .... Include mailing lists news groups and chat groups.

A] Discussion Groups.

B] Internet Groups.

C] IP Groups.

D] All of these.

Q.6. Which of the following is a search engine.

A] Google.

B] Alta Vista.

C] Yahoo.

D] All of these.

Q.7. Directory Search is also known as Index Search.

A] True.

B] False.

Q.8. In IRC, R stands for:

A] Real.

B] Relay.

C] Record.

D] Random.

Q.9. Applets are the special programs written in .... language.

A] Java.

B] HTML.

C] HTTP.

D] None of these.

Q.10. E-mail includes all of the following basic elements except.

A] Header.

B] Footer.

C] Message.

D] Signature.

Q.11. Instant messaging allows you

A] Send E-mail messages.

B] Sharing the data.

C] Instant reply of your messages.

D] To communicate with many at once in a conversation that occurs in real time.

Q.12.] When you use a] n. .... to search for a topic the information you search through is organized into a database - like structure.

A] Search Engine.

B] Index.

C] Spider.
D] Applet.
Q.13. .The extensions .gov, .edu, .mil, and .net are called.
A] DNSs.
B] E-mail targets.
C] Domain codes.
D] Mail to addresses.
Q.14.] Web spider are also known as search engines..
A] True.
B] False.
Q.15.B2c, C2C and B2B are types of...............
A] E-mail.
B] E-commerce.
C] E-cash.
D] All of these.
Q.16. For navigating any website, user has to enter.
A] URL.
B] www.
C] PPP.
D] None of these.
Q.17. Web spiders and Crawlers are examples of
A] Browsers.
B] Search Engines.
C] HTML Programs.
D] Flames.
Q.18. The .com indicates website of .... type of organization.
A] Commerce.
B] Complex.
C] Company.
D] Cargo.
Q.19.ISP stands for.
A] Internal Service Plan.
B] Internet Service Plan.
C] Integral Service Plan.
D] Internet Service Provider.
Q.20............ are programs that provide access to web resources.
A] Browsers.
B] Search Engines.

C] Programs.

D] All of these.

Q.21. Which is a web search engine used World Wide?

A] Domains.

B] Google.

C] Toggle.

D] All of these.

Q.22. Discussion on the internet about specific is known as

A] News.

B] News Group.

C] Veronica.

D] Telnet.

Q.23. Full from of URL

A] Universal Resource Locator.

B] Uniform Resource Locator.

C] Uni Resource Locator.

D] None of these.

Q.24. .... are the special programs written in Java.

A] Java Programs.

B] Applets.

C] Projects.

D] None of these.

Q.25. FTP stands for.

A] Field Transfer Project.

B] File Transfer Project.

C] File Transfer Protocol.

D] None of these.

Q.26. Plug-ins are programs that are automatically started and operate as a part of the browser.

A] True.

B] False.

Q.27. Keyword search is also known as Index search.

A] True.

B] False.

Q.28. When you type an address such as "http://www.mkcl.org," in this. org indicates that it is a

A] Original Web Site.

B] Commercial Web Site.

C] Organizational Web Site.

D] Educational Web Site.

Q.29. You can seach the World Wide Web for a specific topic by using .... and ....

A] Gophers, Fidos.

B] Scanners, Search engine.

C] Search engine, Index.

D] Browsers, Lukers.

Q.30. Mailing lists allow members to communicate by sending messages to a list address.

A] True.

B] False.

Q.31. A popular chat service is called -

A] Internet Release Chat.

B] Internet Request Chat.

C] Internet Resource Chat.

D] Internet Relay Chat.

Q.32. A programming language used for creating applets is called java.

A] True.

B] False.

Q.33. When you use a] n. .... to search for a topic, the information you search through is organized into a database - like structure.

A] Search Engine.

B] Index.

C] Spider.

D] Applet.

Q.34. The last part of the domain name following the dot .. is called as ....

A] Domain Codes.

B] E-mail Targets.

C] DNSs.

D] Mail to addresses.

Q.35. Following is a script language used, while designing a web page.

A] Hyper Text Mark-up Language.

B] Hyper Link Mark-up Language.

C] Hyper Text Web Language.

D] None of these.

Q.36. What is e-mail?

A] Engineering Mailing.

B] Internet Mailing.

C] Electronic Mailing.

D] All of the above.

Q.37. IM stands for ....

A] Instant Making.

B] Internal Messaging.

C] Instant Messaging.

D] None of these.

Q.38.Microsoft's internet explorel is awidely used browser.

A] True.

B] False.

Q.39. Directory search is also known as

A] Direct Search.

B] Unique Search.

C] Index Search.

D] All of these.

Q.40. What is URL

A] A software package used to cruise the World Wide Web.

B] The address of resource on the World Wide Web.

C] The term used to describe an internet wizard.

D] Unlimited Real time language.

Q.41. Netscape Navigator is a type of ....

A] Utility Program.

B] Operating System.

C] Browser.

D] Web Authoring Program.

Q.1........... Programs that guard your computer system against viruses or other damaging programs.

A] Backup.

B] Antivirus.

C] Uninstall.

D] None of these.

Q.2. Multitasking in the ability of the operating system to run more than one application at a time.

A] True.

B] False.

Q.3. .... is a utility program that locates and eliminates unnecessary fragments and rearranges files and unused disk space to optimize operations.

A] Backup.

B] <u>Disk Defragmenter.</u>

C] Uninstall.

D] All of these.

Q.4. Uninstall programs enable removing unneeded programs installed into the computer's hard disk.

A] <u>True.</u>

B] False.

Q.5. Backup programs make copies of the files to be used in case the original files are damaged or lost.

A] <u>True.</u>

B] False.

Q.6............ is the ability of the operating system to run more than one application at a time.

A] Booting.

B] Copping.

C] Pasting.

D] <u>Multitasking.</u>

Q.7............ are used to store data and programs.

A] Folder.

B] <u>File</u>.

C] Recycle bin.

D] None of these.

Q.8. A .... is a connecting ring.

A] <u>Track.</u>

B] Sectors.

C] Round.

D] None of these.

Q.9.The operating system provides the user interface, controls the computers resources, and runs programs.

A] <u>True.</u>

B] False.

Q.10. Each track is divided into wedge-shaped sections called ....

A] Track.

B] <u>Sectors.</u>

C] Round.

D] None of these.

Q.11............ are also known as service programs.

A] OS.

B] Device Drivers.

C] Utilities.

D] All of these.

Q.12. Type of software that can be described as "end user" software.

A] DOS.

B] System Software.

C] Application Software.

D] Operating Software.

Q.13.GUI Stands for

A] Graphical User Interface.

B] Greater User Interface.

C] Graphical Union Interface.

D] Graphical User Interface.

Q.14. Which of these operating system does not have a graphical user interface ?

A] Windows 95.

B] Mac OS.

C] Linux.

D] MS DOS.

Q.15. Language translators convert the programming instructions, written by programmers into a language that computer understand and process.

A] True.

B] False.

Q.16............ is a collection of several separate troubleshooting utilities.

A] Backup.

B] Norton Utilities.

C] Uninstall.

D] All of the above.

Q.17. .... provides the user interface, controls the computers resources, and runs programs.

A] Drivers.

B] Operating System.

C] Desktop.

D] None of these.

Q.18............ utility identifies non essential files on the hard disk and erases them only when user allows their erasure.

A] Uninstall Program.

B] Backup.

C] File Compression.

D] Disk Clean up.

Q.19. Which of the following is the function of operating system.

A] Managing Resources.

B] Running Applications.

C] Providing User Interface.

D] All of the Above.

Q.20. .... are graphical objects used to represent commonly used applications.

A] GUI.

B] Drivers.

C] Windows NT.

D] Icons.

Q.21. Starting or re-starting a computer is called............. The system.

A] Booting.

B] Copping.

C] Pasting.

D] Multitasking.

Q.22. .... are specialized programs that allow particular input or output devices to communicate with the rest of the computer system.

A] Device Drivers.

B] Utilities.

C] OS.

D] None of these.

Q.23. Disk Defragmenter is a utility program, that locates and eliminates unnecessary fragments and rearranges files and unused disk space to optimize operations.

A] True.

B] False.

Q.24. The .... displays a list of commands that can be used to gain access to information, change hardware settings, find information stored in the, get online help and shut down the computer.

A] GUI.

B] Desktop.

C] Icon.

D] Start Button.

Q.25. Which of the following example of network operating systems ?

A] Netware.

B] Windows N.T. Server.

C] Windows XP Server.

D] All of the above.

Q.26. Utilities are also known as service programs

A] True.

B] False.

Q.27. Which programs reduce the size of the files so that they occupy lesser space on the disk.

A] Backup.

B] Disk Cleanup.

C] File Compression.

D] Uninstall Program.

Q.28. Each track is divided into wedge-shaped called sectors.

A] True.

B] False.

Q.29. Starting or Restarting a computer is called multitasking the system.

A] True.

B] False.

Q.30. .... convert the programming instruction written by programmers into a language that computers understand and process.

A] Utilities.

B] Device Drivers.

C] Language Translators.

D] None of these.

Q.31. System software includes all of the following except.

A] Operating System.

B] Device Drivers.

C] Utilities.

D] Desktop Publishing.

Q.32. .... is background software that helps the computer manage its own internal resources.

A] System Software.

B] Information.

C] Objects.

D] None of these.

Q.33. Operating systems are programs that manage resource, provide user interface and run applications.

A] True.

B] False.

Q.34. Starting or Re-starting a computer is called booting the system.

A] True.

B] False.

Q.35. Antivirus programs are meant to guard a computer from invasion of the virus programs.

A] True.

B] False.

Q.36. Uninstall programs enable removing unneeded programs on started into

A] True.

B] False.

Q.37. Trouble shooting programs recognize both hardware and software problems and try to correct them as far as possible.

A] True.

B] False.

Q.38. Device Drivers are specialized programs that allow particular input or output devices to communicate with the rest computer system.

A] True.

B] False.

Q.39. Antivirus programs are meant to guard a computer from invasion of the virus programs.

A] True.

B] False.

Q.1. Microprocessor has two basic components.

A] Control Unit.

B] Arithmetic Logic Unit.

C] All of these.

D] None of these.

Q.2. Which of the following is a data processing unit

A] CPU.

B] RAM.

C] Hard Disk.

D] Floppy.

Q.3.Fire-Wire port is also called as High Performance Serial Bus HPSB. Port.

A] True.

B] False.

Q.4. Cache memory is used to store most frequently accessed information from the RAM.

A] True.

B] False.

Q.5. RISC stands for.

A] Reduced Instruction Set Computer.

B] Read Instruction Set Computer.

C] Reduce Instruction Software Computer.

D] None of these.

Q.6. The........... Connects all system computers and allows input and output device to communicate with the system unit.

A] System Board.

B] Monitor.

C] Mouse.

D] None of these.

Q.7. The types of microprocessor chips are

A] CISC Chips.

B] RISC Chips.

C] All of these.

D] None of these.

Q.8. Data transfer through a serial port is faster than that of a parallel port.

A] True.

B] False.

Q.9. Which of following is a primary memory ?

A] RAM.

B] CD.

C] Floppy.

D] Hard Disk.

Q.10. Random Access Memory] RAM. is .... type of memory.

A] Permanent.

B] Temporary.

C] Flash.

D] Smart.

Q.11. ASCII, EBCDIC and Unicode are examples of Application Software.

A] True.

B] False.

Q.12. Eight bits makes up a bite.

A] True.

B] False.

Q.13. In a microprocessor system, the Central Processing Unit C.P.U. Or a processor is contained on a single chip called the microprocessor.

A] True.

B] False.

Q.14. CISC stands for.

A] Computer Instruction Set Computer.

B] Complex Instruction Set Computer.

C] Complex Index Set Computer.

D] None of these.

Q.15. ASCII, EBCDIC and Unicode are binery coding schemes.

A] True.

B] False.

Q.16. Note book system units are often called as ....

A] PDA.

B] Laptop.

C] Desktop.

D] None of these.

Q.17. .... is also known as the system cabinet or chassis.

A] System Unit.

B] Monitor.

C] Key board.

D] None of these.

Q.18. Data stored in Flash RAM does not get erased even when power to the computer is switched off.

A] True.

B] False.

Q.19. The system board is also known as the main board or mother board.

A] True.

B] False.

Q.20. Capacity of a storage device is usually measured in terms of bytes.

A] True.

B] False.

Q.21. Which of the following component is used to store data?

A] CPU.

B] Memory.

C] Input Device.

D] Output Device.

Q.22. Microprocessor is often called a CPU.

A] True.

B] False.

Q.23. In a microprocessor system, the control processing unit] C.P.U.. or processor is contained on a single chip called the ....

A] Slot.

B] Port.

C] Microprocessor.

D] None of these.

Q.24. .... is a 16-bit code designed to support international language like Chinese and Japanese.

A] Unicode.

B] ASSCII

C] EBCDIC

D] None of these.

Q.26. Which of the following is the unit of computer memory.

A] Kilogram.

B] Kilobytes.

A] Meter.

B] Celsius.

Q.27. Parallel ports are mostly used to connect printers to the system unit.

A] True.

B] False.

Q.28. Data and instructions are represented electronically with a binary or two-state numbering system.

A] True.

B] False.

Q.29. Which of the following is the highest unit of memory ?

A] Gigabyte.

B] Bytes.

C] Megabytes.

D] Kilobytes.

Q.30. The system board connects all system components and allow input and output device to communicate with the system unit.

A] <u>True.</u>

B] False.

Q.31. In parallel port data is transmitted one byte after another.

A] <u>True.</u>

B] False.

Q.32. Which of the following is a primary memory?

A] <u>RAM.</u>

B] CD.

C] Floppy.

D] Hard Disk.

Q.33. Socrates, slots and bus lines are components of the system board.

A] <u>True.</u>

B] False.

Q.34. Each 0 and 1 in the binary numbering system is called a bit.

A] <u>True.</u>

B] False.

Q.1. Output of an image on the monitor screen is often called hard copy.

A] True.

B] <u>False.</u>

Q.2. MIRC can be used to read data from checks in a bank.

A] <u>True.</u>

B] False.

Q.3. A monitor with resolution of 800 x 600 has 800 pixels horizontally and 600 pixels vertically.

A] <u>True.</u>

B] False.

Q.4. The keys labelled 0 -9 on the keyboard are called.

A] Function Keys.

B] Typewriters Keys.

C] <u>Numeric Keys.</u>

D] Special purpose Keys.

Q.5. The functions of a mouse and a track ball are different.

A] True.

B] False.

Q.6. .... devices translate what people understand into a form that computers can process.

A] Input.

B] Output.

A] All of these.

B] None of these.

Q.7. The keyboards keys that are labelled F1, F2 and so on are called................

A] Function Keys.

B] Numeric Keys.

C] Typewriter Keys.

D] Special Purpose Key.

Q.8. Which of the following device is not from pointing type of device?

A] Mouse.

B] Touch screen.

C] Key board.

D] Joystick.

Q.9. which of these is not a input device?

A] Monitor.

B] Mouse.

C] Key board.

D] Joystick.

Q.10. OCR is used to translate printed text to machine readable code.

A] True.

B] False.

Q.11. Optical character recognition device and optical mark recognition device are two names of the same device.

A] True.

B] False.

Q.12. Aspect ratio of a monitor is the ratio of number of horizontal pixels to number of vertical pixels.

A] True.

B] False.

Q.13. Output of an image on the monitor screen is often called a hardcopy.

A] True.

B False.

Q.14. The keyboard keys like caps lock that turn a feature on or off are called.

A] Function Keys.

B] Combination Keys.

C] Toggle Keys.

D] Special Purpose Keys.

Q.15. Primary function of a monitor is to display information to the user.

A] True.

B] False.

Q.16. Headphone is a typical output device.

A] True.

B] False.

Q.17. The mouse pointer seen on the desktop is also called as...............

A] Arrow Pointer.

B] Key Pointer.

C] Display Pointer.

D] None of these.

Q.18. Plotters are used to produce special purpose graphics.

A] True.

B] False.

Q.19. Input device translate what people understand into a form that computers can process.

A] True.

B] False.

Q.20. Primary function of a common keyboard in a computer is to play music like a piano.

A] True.

B] False.

Q.21. The easiest way to access any part of the screen in the windows operating system is using the

A] Key board.

B] Rat.

C] Mouse.

D] Joystick.

Q.22. Dot matrix printers make irritating noise.

A] True.

B] False.

Q.23. Joystick is very useful in playing speed games.

A] <u>True.</u>

B] False.

Q.24. Printers can be connected to a computer for producing output on a paper.

A] <u>True.</u>

B] False.

Q.25. Instead of function keys which are use to create a shortcut.

A] Toggle Keys.

B] Special Keys.

C] <u>Combination Keys.</u>

D] Numeric Keys.

Q.26. Method of working of a flatbed scanner is mostly similar to a photocopying machine.

A] <u>True.</u>

B] False.

Q.27. Output of an image on the monitor screen is often called soft copy.

A] <u>True.</u>

B] False.

Q.28. Which printer print data or image by spraying small drops of ink at high speed into the surface of the paper ?

A] <u>Ink Jet Printer.</u>

B] Laser Printer.

C] Dot Matrix Printer.

D] Drum Printer.

Q.29. Which of the following key is not a toggle key ?

A] Caps Lock.

B] Num Lock.

C] Scroll Lock.

D] <u>Control.</u>

Q.30. The keyboard keys that have arrows on them are called.

A] Function Keys.

B] <u>Navigation Keys.</u>

C] Typewriters Keys.

D] Special Purpose Keys.

Q.31. A .... is a light sensitive pen like device.

A] <u>Light Pen</u>.

B] Joy Stick.

C] Touch Screen.

D] None of these.

Q.32. Output of an image through a printer is often called hard copy.

A] True.

B] False.

Q.33. which of the following device is used to play fast computer games?

A] Joystick.

B] Touch Surface.

C] Touch Screen.

D] Track Ball.

Q.1. A track on a disk is the one of the many circular ring shaped areas where data is written magnetically.

A] True.

B] False.

Q.2. Which of these is not a file compressing program ?

A] Win Zip.

B] PK Zip.

C] Win RAR.

D] RAID.

Q.3. The traditional floppy disk is the 1.44 MB 3.5 inch disk.

A] True.

B] False.

Q.4. .... disk from the Sony Corporation have a capacity of 200 MB or 720 MB.

A] Super Disk.

B] HiFD Disk.

C] Zip Disk.

D] None of these.

Q.5. High capacity disks also known as floppy disk cartridges are rapidly replacing the traditional floppy disk.

A] True.

B] False.

Q.6. .... improves hard-disk performance by anticipating data needs.

A] Disk Catching.

B] Disk Defragment.

C] Disk Writing.

D] None of these.

Q.7. 3.5 floppy disk capacity is ....

A] 1.44 MB.

B] 1 MB.

C] 1.66 MB.

D] 1.55 MB.

Q.8. Super disks are produced by Imation and have a 120 MB or 240 MB capacity.

A] True.

B] False.

Q.9. A CD-ROM stands for.

A] Compact Disk Read Only Memory.

B] Compact Disk Read Once Memory.

C] CD-RW.

D] None of these.

Q.10........... Programs that guard your computer system against viruses or other damaging programs.

A] Backup.

B] Anti Virus.

C] Uninstall.

D] None of these.

Q.11. What is the name given to a part of circle on which data is written in a storage media ?

A] Track.

B] Sector.

C] Cylinder.

D] Spiral.

Q.12. A CD-RW Disk means.

A] CD-Rewriteable.

B] CD-Recordable.

C] CD-ROM.

D] None of these.

Q.13. .... are produced by omega and topically have a 100 MB, 250 MB or 750 MB capacity over 500 times as much as today's standard floppy disk.

A] Super Disk.

B] HiFD Disk.

C] Zip Disk.

D] None of these.

Q.14. Primary storage is a volatile.

A] True.

B] False.

Q.15. HiFD Disks from the Sony Corporation have a capacity of 200 MB or 720 MB.

A] True.

B] False.

Q.16........... are produced by Imation and have a 120 MB or 240 MB capacity.

A] Super Disk.

B] HiFD Disk.

C] Zip Disk.

D] None of these.

Q.17. .... are removable storage devices used to store massive amounts of information.

A] Hard Disk Packs.

B] C.D..

C] Floppy Disk.

D] None of these.

Q.18. each track is divided into wedge-shaped sections called sectors.

A] True.

B] False.

Q.19. Storage device are hardware that reads data and programs from storage media.

A] True.

B] False.

Q.20. The 2 HD on a disk label means.

A] Two side, Low Density.

B] Two Side High Density.

C] One Side High Density.

D] None of these.

Q.21............ disks have a 120 MB storage capacity and the drivers are also able to read and store data on a standard 3.5" floppy disk.

A] Super Disks.

B] HiFD Disks.

C] Zip Disks.

D] None of these.

Q.22. Zip disks are produced by omega and typically have a 100 MB, 250 MB or 750 MB capacity over 500 times such as much as today's standard floppy disks.

A] True.

B] False.

Q.23. A CD-R stands for.

A] CD-Recordable.

B] CD-Runner.

C] CD-Receiver.

D] None of these.

Q.24. Each track is divided into wedge-shaped sections called.

A] Track.

B] Sectors.

C] Round.

D] None of these.

Q.25. Hard disk packs are removable storage devices used to massive amounts of information.

A] True.

B] False.

Q.26. Secondary Storage is non-volatile.

A] True.

B] False.

Q.27. Floppy disks are removable storage media.

A] True.

B] False.

1] Awebpage displays a picture] What tag was used to display that picture?

a] picture

b] image

c]img

d] src

2] <b> tag makes the enclosed text bold] What is other tag to make text bold?

a] <strong>

b] <dar>

c] <black>

d] <emp>

3] Tags and test that are not directly displayed on the page are written in _____ section]

a] <html>

b] <head>

c] <title>
d] <body>
4] Which tag inserts a line horizontally on your web page?
a] <hr>
b] <line>
c] <line direction="horizontal">
d] <tr>
5] What should be the first tag in any HTML document?
a] <head>
b] <title>
c] <html>
d] <document>
6] Which tag allows you to add a row in a table?
a] <td> and </td>
b] <cr> and </cr>
c] <th> and </th>
d] <tr> and </tr>
7] How can you make a bulleted list?
a] <list>
b] <nl>
c] <ul>
d] <ol>
8] How can you make a numbered list?
a] <dl>
b] <ol>
c] <list>
d] <ul>
9] How can you make an e-mail link?
a] <a href="xxx@yyy">
b] <mail href="xxx@yyy">
c] <mail>xxx@yyy</mail>
d] <a href="mailto:xxx@yyy">
10] What is the correct HTML for making a hyperlink?
a] <a href="http:// mcqsets]com">ICT Trends Quiz</a>
b] <a name="http://mcqsets]com">ICT Trends Quiz</a>
c] <http://mcqsets]com</a>
d] url="http://mcqsets]com">ICT Trends Quiz
11] Choose the correct HTML tag to make a text italic

a] <ii>
b] <italics>
c] <italic>
d] <i>
12] Choose the correct HTML tag to make a text bold?
a] <b>
b] <bold>
c] <bb>
d] <bld>
13] What is the correct HTML for adding a background color?
a] <body color="yellow">
b] <body bgcolor="yellow">
c] <background>yellow</background>
d] <body background="yellow">
14] Choose the correct HTML tag for the smallest size heading?
a] <heading>
b] <h6>
c] <h1>
d] <head>
15] What is the correct HTML tag for inserting a line break?
a]
b] <lb>
c] <break>
d] <newline>
16] What doesvlink attribute mean?
a] visited link
b] virtual link
c] very good link
d] active link
17] Which attribute is used to name an element uniquely?
a] class
b] id
c] dot
d] all of above
18] Which tag creates a check box for a form in HTML?
a] <checkbox>
b] <input type="checkbox">
c] <input=checkbox>

d] <input checkbox>
19] To create a combo box (drop down box) which tag will you use?
a] <select>
b] <list>
c] <input type="dropdown">
d] all of above
20] Which of the following is not a pair tag?
a] <p>
b] < u >
c] <i>
d] <img>
21] To create HTML document you requirea
a] web page editing software
b] High powered computer
c] Just a notepad can be used
d] None of above
22] The special formatting codes in HTML document used to present contentare
a] tags
b] attributes
c] values
d] None of above
23] HTML documents are saved in
a] Special binary format
b] Machine language codes
c] ASCII text
d] None of above
24] Some tags enclose the text] Those tags are known as
a] Couple tags
b] Single tags
c] Double tags
d] Pair tags
25] The ______ character tells browsers to stop tagging the text
a] ?
b] /
c] >
d] %
26] In HTML document the tags

a] Should be written in upper case
b] should be written in lower case
c] should be written in propercase
d] can be written in both uppercase or lowercase
27] Marquee is a tag in HTML to
a] mark the list of items to maintaininqueue
b] Mark the text so that it is hidden in browser
c] Display text with scrolling effect
d] None of above
28] There are _____ different of heading tags in HTML
a] 4
b] 5
c] 6
d] 7
29] To create a blank line in your web page
a] press Enter two times
b] press Shift + Enter
c] insert <BR> tag
d] insert <BLINE>
30] Which of the following is not a style tag?
a] <b>
b] <tt>
c] <i>
d] All of above are style tags
31] The way the browser displays the object can be modified by ______
a] attributes
b] parameters
c] modifiers
d] None of above
32] Which of the following HTML code is valid?
a] <font colour="red">
b] <font color="red">
c] <red><font>
d] All of above are style tags
33] Which of the following is an attribute related to font tag?
a] size
b] face
c] color

d] <u>All of above are style tags</u>

34] HTML supports

a] ordered lists

b] unordered lists

c] <u>both type of lists</u>

d] does not support those types

35] What tag is used to list individual items of an ordered list?

a] <u>LI</u>

b] OL

c] UL

d] None of above

36] When should you use path along with file name of picture in IMG tag?

a] path is optional and not necessary

b] <u>when the location of image file andhtml file are different</u>

c] when image file andhtml file both are on same location

d] path is always necessary when inserting image

37] Which of the following is not a valid alignment attribute?

a] Left

b] Right

c] <u>Top</u>

d] All of above

38] Which attribute is used withimg tag to display the text if image could not load in browser?

a] description

b] name

c] <u>alt</u>

d] id

39] Which attribute can be used with BODY tag to set background color green?

a] background="green"

b] <u>bgcolor="green"</u>

c] vlink="green"

d] None of above

40] Which attribute you'll use with TD tag to merge two cells horizontally?

a] merge=colspan2

b] rowspan=2

c] <u>colspan=2</u>

d] merge=row2

41] Awebpage displays a picture] What tag was used to display that picture?

a] picture

b]mage

c]<u>img</u>

d] src

42] <b> tag makes the enclosed text bold] What is other tag to make text bold?

a] <u><strong></u>

b] <dar>

c] <black>

d] <emp>

43] Tags and test that are not directly displayed on the page are written in ______ section]

a] <html>

b] <u><head></u>

c] <title>

d] <body>

44] Which tag inserts a line horizontally on your web page?

a] <u><hr></u>

b] <line>

c] <line direction="horizontal">

d] <tr>

45] What should be the first tag in any HTML document?

a] <head>

b] <title>

c] <u><html></u>

d] <document>

46] Which tag allows you to add a row in a table?

a] <td> and </td>

b] <cr> and </cr>

c] <th> and </th>

d] <u><tr> and </tr></u>

47] How can you make a bulleted list?

a] <list>

b] <nl>

c] <ul>
d] <ol>
48] How can you make a numbered list?
a] <dl>
b] <ol>
c] <list>
d] <ul>
49] How can you make an e-mail link?
a] <a href="xxx@yyy">
b] <mail href="xxx@yyy">
c] <mail>xxx@yyy</mail>
d] <a href="mailto:xxx@yyy">
50] What is the correct HTML for making a hyperlink?
a] <a href="http://mcqsets]com">MCQ Sets Quiz</a>
b] <a name="http://mcqsets]com">MCQ Sets Quiz</a>
c] <http://mcqsets]com</a>
d] url="http://mcqsets]com">MCQ Sets Quiz
1) CSS stands for -
A] Cascade style sheets
B] Color and style sheets
C] Cascading style sheets
D] None of the above
2) Which of the following is the correct syntax for referring the external style sheet?
A] <style src = example.css>
B] <style src = "example.css" >
C] <stylesheet> example.css </stylesheet>
D] <link rel="stylesheet" type="text/css" href="example.css">
3) The property in CSS used to change the background color of an element is -
A] bgcolor
B] color
C] background-color
D] All of the above
4) The property in CSS used to change the text color of an element is -
A] bgcolor
B] color
C] background-color

D] All of the above

Hide Answer Workspace

5) The CSS property used to control the element's font-size is -

A] text-style

B] text-size

C] font-size

D] None of the above

6) The HTML attribute used to define the inline styles is -

A] style

B] styles

C] class

D] None of the above

7) The HTML attribute used to define the internal stylesheet is -

A] <style>

B] style

C] <link>

D] <script>

8) Which of the following CSS property is used to set the background image of an element?

A] background-attachment

B] background-image

C] background-color

D] None of the above

9) Which of the following is the correct syntax to make the background-color of all paragraph elements to yellow?

A] p {background-color : yellow;}

B] p {background-color : #yellow;}

C] all {background-color : yellow;}

D] all p {background-color : #yellow;}

10) Which of the following is the correct syntax to display the hyperlinks without any underline?

A] a {text-decoration : underline;}

B] a {decoration : no-underline;}

C] a {text-decoration : none;}

D] None of the above

11) Which of the following property is used as the shorthand property for the padding properties?

A] padding-left

B] padding-right
C] padding
D] All of the above

12) The CSS property used to make the text bold is -
A] font-weight : bold
B] weight: bold
C] font: bold
D] style: bold

13) Are the negative values allowed in padding property?
A] Yes
B] No
C] Can't say
D] May be

14) Which of the following property is used as the shorthand property of margin properties?
A] margin-left
B] margin-right
C] margin
D] None of the above

15) The CSS property used to specify the transparency of an element is -
A] opacity
B] filter
C] visibility
D] overlay

16) Which of the following is used to specify the subscript of text using CSS?
A] vertical-align: sub
B] vertical-align: super
C] vertical-align: subscript
D] of the above

17) Which of the following CSS property is used to specify the space between every letter inside an element?
A] alpha-spacing
B] character-spacing
C] letter-spacing
D] alphabet-spacing

18) The CSS property used to specify whether the text is written in the horizontal or vertical direction?

A] writing-mode

B] text-indent

C] word-break

D] None of the above

19) Which of the following syntax is correct in CSS to make each word of a sentence start with a capital letter?

A] text-style : capital;

B] transform : capitalize;

C] text-transform : capital;

D] text-transform : capitalize;

20) How to select the elements with the class name "example"?

A] example

B] #example

C] .example

D] Class example

21) Which of the following is the correct syntax to select all paragraph elements in a div element?

A] div p

B] p

C] div#p

D] div ~ p

22) Which of the following is the correct syntax to select the p siblings of a div element?

A] p

B] div + p

C] div p

D] div ~ p

23) The CSS property used to draw a line around the elements outside the border?

A] border

B] outline

C] padding

D] line

24) Which of the following CSS property is used to add shadows to the text?

A] text-shadow

B] text-stroke

C] text-overflow

D] text-decoration

25) Which of the following is not a value of the font-variant property in CSS?

A] normal

B] small-caps

C] large-caps

D] inherit

26) Which of the following CSS property is used to specify whether the table cells share the common or separate border?

A] border-collapse

B] border-radius

C] border-spacing

D] None of the above

27) The CSS property used to make the rounded borders, or rounded corners around an element is -

A] border-collapse

B] border-radius

C] border-spacing

D] None of the above

28) The CSS property used to set the distance between the borders of the adjacent cells in the table is -

A] border-collapse

B] border-radius

C] border-spacing

D] None of the above

29) Which of the following selector in CSS is used to select the elements that do not match the selectors?

A] :! selector

B] :not selector

C] :empty selector

D] None of the above

30) Which of the following is not a type of combinator?

A] >

B] ~

C] +

D] *

31) Which of the following CSS property defines how an image or video fits into container with established height and width?

A] object-fit

B] object-position

C] position

D] None of the above

32) Which type of CSS is used in the below code?

<p style = "border:2px solid red;">

A] Inline CSS

B] Internal CSS

C] External CSS

D] None of the above

33) Which of the following CSS property specifies the origin of the background-image?

A] background-origin

B] background-attachment

C] background-size

D] None of the above

34) The CSS property used to set the maximum width of the element's content box is -

A] max-width property

B] height property

C] max-height property

D] position property

35) Which if the following CSS function allows us to perform calculations?

A] calc() function

B] calculator() function

C] calculate() function

D] cal() function

36) The CSS property used to set the maximum height of the element's content box is -

A] max-width property

B] height property

C] max-height property

D] position property

37) The CSS property used to set the minimum width of the element's content box is -

A] max-width property

B] min-width property

C] width property

D] All of the above

38) Which of the following CSS property is used to represent the overflowed text which is not visible to the user?

A] text-shadow

B] text-stroke

C] text-overflow

D] text-decoration

39) The CSS property which is used to define the set the difference between two lines of your content is -

A] min-height property

B] max-height property

C] line-height property

D] None of the above

40) The CSS property which is used to define the set the difference between two lines of your content is -

A] min-height property

B] max-height property

C] line-height property

D] None of the above

41) Which of the following CSS property is used to add stroke to the text?

A] text-stroke property

B] text-transform property

C] text-decoration property

D] None of the above

42) Which of the following CSS property is used to set the blend mode for each background layer of an element?

A] background-blend-mode property

B] background-collapse property

C] background-transform property

D] background-origin property

43) The CSS property used to specify the transparency of an element is -

A] Hover

B] opacity

C] clearfix

D] overlay

44) Which of the following CSS property is used to set the horizontal alignment of a table-cell box or the block element?

A] text-align property

B] text-transform property

C] text-shadow property

D] text-decoration

45) The CSS property which is used to set the text wider or narrower compare to the default width of the font is -

A] font-stretch property

B] font-weight property

C] text-transform property

D] font-variant property

46) Which of the following CSS property is used to specify the type of quotation mark?

A] quotes property

B] z-index property

C] hyphens property

D] None of the above

47) The CSS property used to specify the order of flex item in the grid container is -

A] order property

B] float property

C] overflow property

D] None of the above

48) The CSS property used to set the indentation of the first line in a block of text is -

A] text-indent property

B] text-stroke property

C] text-decoration property

D] text-overflow property

49) Which of the following CSS property creates a clipping region and specifies the visible area of the element?

A] visibility property

B] background-clip property

C] clip-path property

D] None of the above

50) The correct syntax to give a line over text is -

A] text-decoration: line-through

B] text-decoration: none

C] text-decoration: overline

D] text-decoration: underline

1] Why so JavaScript and Java have similar name?

A] JavaScript is a stripped-down version of Java

B] JavaScript's syntax is loosely based on Java's

C] They both originated on the island of Java

D] None of the above

2] When a user views a page containing a JavaScript program, which machine actually executes the script?

A] The User's machine running a Web browser

B] The Web server

C] A central machine deep within Netscape's corporate offices

D] None of the above

3] _______ JavaScript is also called client-side JavaScript]

A] Microsoft

B] Navigator

C] LiveWire

D] Native

4] ___________ JavaScript is also called server-side JavaScript]

A] Microsoft

B] Navigator

C] LiveWire

D] Native

5] What are variables used for in JavaScript Programs?

A] Storing numbers, dates, or other values

B] Varying randomly

C] Causing high-school algebra flashbacks

D] None of the above

6] ______ JavaScript statements embedded in an HTML page can respond to user events such as mouse-clicks, form input, and page navigation]

A] Client-side

B] Server-side

C] Local

D] Native

7] What should appear at the very end of your JavaScript?

The <script LANGUAGE="JavaScript">tag
A] The </script>
B] The <script>
C] The END statement
D] None of the above
8] Which of the following can't be done with client-side JavaScript?
A] Validating a form
B] Sending a form's contents by email
C] Storing the form's contents to a database file on the server
D] None of the above
9] Which of the following are capabilities of functions in JavaScript?
A] Return a value
B] Accept parameters and Return a value
C] Accept parameters
D] None of the above
10] Which of the following is not a valid JavaScript variable name?
A] 2names
B] _first_and_last_names
C] FirstAndLast
D] None of the above
11] _______ tag is an extension to HTML that can enclose any number of JavaScript statements]
A] <SCRIPT>
B] <BODY>
C] <HEAD>
D] <TITLE>
12] How does JavaScript store dates in a date object?
A] The number of milliseconds since January 1st, 1970
B] The number of days since January 1st, 1900
C] The number of seconds since Netscape's public stock offering]
D] None of the above
13] Which of the following attribute can hold the JavaScript version?
A] LANGUAGE
B] SCRIPT
C] VERSION
D] None of the above
14] What is the correct JavaScript syntax to write "Hello World"?
A] System]out]println("Hello World")

B] println ("Hello World")

C] document]write("Hello World")

D] response]write("Hello World")

15] Which of the following way can be used to indicate the LANGUAGE attribute?

A] <LANGUAGE="JavaScriptVersion">

B] <SCRIPT LANGUAGE="JavaScriptVersion">

C] <SCRIPT LANGUAGE="JavaScriptVersion"> JavaScript statements...</SCRIPT>

D] <SCRIPT LANGUAGE="JavaScriptVersion"!> JavaScript statements...</SCRIPT>

16] Inside which HTML element do we put the JavaScript?

A] <js>

B] <scripting>

C] <script>

D] <javascript>

17] What is the correct syntax for referring to an external script called " abc]js"?

A] <script href=" abc]js">

B] <script name=" abc]js">

C] <script src=" abc]js">

D] None of the above

18] Which types of image maps can be used with JavaScript?

A] Server-side image maps

B] Client-side image maps

C] Server-side image maps and Client-side image maps

D] None of the above

19] Which of the following navigator object properties is the same in both Netscape and IE?

A] navigator]appCodeName

B] navigator]appName

C] navigator]appVersion

D] None of the above

20] Which is the correct way to write a JavaScript array?

A] var txt = new Array(1:"tim",2:"kim",3:"jim")

B] var txt = new Array:1=("tim")2=("kim")3=("jim")

C] var txt = new Array("tim","kim","jim")

D] var txt = new Array="tim","kim","jim"

21] What does the <noscript> tag do?

A] Enclose text to be displayed by non-JavaScript browsers

B] Prevents scripts on the page from executing

C] Describes certain low-budget movies

D] None of the above

22] If para1 is the DOM object for a paragraph, what is the correct syntax to change the text within the paragraph?

A] "New Text"?

B] para1]value="New Text";

C] para1]firstChild]nodeValue= "New Text";

D] para1]nodeValue="New Text";

23] JavaScript entities start with ________ and end with __________

A] Semicolon, colon

B] Semicolon, Ampersand

C] Ampersand, colon

D] Ampersand, semicolon

24] Which of the following best describes JavaScript?

A] a low-level programming language

B] a scripting language precompiled in the browser

C] a compiled scripting language

D] an object-oriented scripting language

25] Choose the server-side JavaScript object?

A] FileUpLoad

B] Function

C] File

D] Date

26] Choose the client-side JavaScript object?

A] Database

B] Cursor

C] Client

D] File UpLoad

27] Which of the following is not considered a JavaScript operator?

A] new

B] this

C] delete

D] typeof

28] _______method evaluates a string of JavaScript code in the context of the specified object]

A] Eval

B] ParseInt

C] ParseFloat

D] Efloat

29] Which of the following event fires when the form element loses the focus: <button>, <input>, <label>, <select>, <textarea>?

A] onfocus

B] onblur

C] onclick

D] ondblclick

30] The syntax of Eval is ________________

A] [objectName]eval(numeric)

B] [objectName]eval(string)

C] [EvalName]eval(string)

D] [EvalName]eval(numeric)

31] JavaScript is interpreted by _________

A] Client

B] Server

C] Object

D] None of the above

32] Using _______ statement is how you test for a specific condition]

A] Select

B] If

C] Switch

D] For

33] Which of the following is the structure of an if statement?

A] if (conditional expression is true) thenexecute this codeend if

B] if (conditional expression is true)execute this codeend if

C] if (conditional expression is true) {then execute this code>->}

D] if (conditional expression is true) then {execute this code}

34] How to create a Date object in JavaScript?

A] dateObjectName = new Date([parameters])

B] dateObjectName.new Date([parameters])

C] dateObjectName := new Date([parameters])

D] dateObjectName Date([parameters])

35] The _______ method of an Array object adds and/or removes elements from an array]

A] Reverse

B] Shift

C] Slice

D] Splice

36] To set up the window to capture all Click events, we use which of the following statement?

A] window.captureEvents(Event.CLICK);

B] window.handleEvents (Event.CLICK);

C] window.routeEvents(Event.CLICK);

D] window.raiseEvents(Event.CLICK);

37] Which tag(s) can handle mouse events in Netscape?

A] <IMG>

B] <A>

C]

D] None of the above

38] ____________ is the tainted property of a window object

A] Pathname

B] Protocol

C] Defaultstatus

D] Host

39] To enable data tainting, the end user sets the _________ environment variable]

A] ENABLE_TAINT

B] MS_ENABLE_TAINT

C] NS_ENABLE_TAINT

D] ENABLE_TAINT_NS

40] In JavaScript, _________ is an object of the target language data type that encloses an object of the source language]

A] a wrapper

B] a link

C] a cursor

D] a form

41] When a JavaScript object is sent to Java, the runtime engine creates a Java wrapper of type ___________

A] ScriptObject

B] JSObject

C] JavaObject

D] Jobject

42] ________ class provides an interface for invoking JavaScript methods and examining JavaScript properties]

A] ScriptObject

B] JSObject

C] JavaObject

D] Jobject

43] __________ is a wrapped Java array, accessed from within JavaScript code]

A] JavaArray

B] JavaClass

C] JavaObject

D] JavaPackage

44] A _________ object is a reference to one of the classes in a Java package, such as netscape]javascript]

A] JavaArray

B] JavaClass

C] JavaObject

D] JavaPackage

45] The JavaScript exception is available to the Java code as an instance of ___________

A] netscape.javascript.JSObject

B] netscape.javascript.JSException

C] netscape.plugin.JSException

D] None of the above

46] To automatically open the console when a JavaScript error occurs which of the following is added to prefs]js?

A] user_pref(" javascript]console]open_on_error", false);

B] user_pref("javascript.console]open_error ", true);

C] user_pref("javascript.console]open_error ", false);

D] user_pref("javascript.console]open_on_error", true);

47] To open a dialog box each time an error occurs, which of the following is added to prefs]js?

A] user_pref("javascript]classic.error_alerts", true);

B] user_pref("javascript]classic.error_alerts ", false);

C] user_pref("javascript]console.open_on_error ", true);

D] user_pref("javascript]console.open_on_error ", false);

48] The syntax of a blur method in a button object is ________________

A] Blur()

B] Blur(contrast)
C] Blur(value)
D] Blur(depth)
49] The syntax of capture events method for document object is ________________

A] captureEvents()
B] captureEvents(args eventType)
C] <u>captureEvents(eventType)</u>
D] captureEvents(eventVal)
50] The syntax of close method for document object is ________________
A] Close(doC]
B] Close(object)
C] Close(val)
D] <u>Close()</u>
1] The programming environment which permits coding, compilation, running and debugging from a single window is called
(a) <u>Integrated Development Environment (IDE)</u>
(b) Editor
(c) Highlighter
(d) Compiler
2] The IDE of VBA supports since it permits drag and drop approach for design of user interface
(a) Procedural Approach
(b) reverse approach
(c) <u>Rapid Application Development (RAD)</u>
(d) postfix approach
3] VBA permits of data from spreadsheets
(a) reading
(b) writing
(c) <u>both reading and writing</u>
(d) neither reading nor writing
4] VBA supports ready made user interface components like
(a) UserForm, CommandButton
(b) Label, TextBox, ComboBox, ListBox
(c) TabStrip, OptionButton, ToggleButton
(d) <u>all of them</u>
5] VBA supports through class module
(a) <u>Object Oriented Programming System (OOPS)</u>

(b) Procedural programming
(c) Functional programming
(d) property based model

6] VBA can be used to automate carried out through MS Excel
(a) data processing
(b) graphing
(c) accessing cell values
(d) all of them

7] VBA code is compiled into an intermediate code called code
(a) P-Code
(b) MicroSoft Intermediate Code (MSIL)
(c) Java Virtual Machine (JVM) code
(d) Android Virtual Device (AVD) code

8] MS Excel creates to execute VBA code
(a) real time computer
(b) mobile computer
(c) tablet computer
(d) virual machine

9] ____is the shortcut to open VBA IDE from MS Excel
(a) Alt+F11
(b) Alt+F8
(c) Ctrl+Break
(d) Ctrl+G

10]_______ is the shortcut to open immediate window in VBA IDE
(a) Alt+F11
(b) Alt+F8
(c) Ctrl+Break
(d) Ctrl+G

11] _______is the shortcut to open list of macros
(a) Alt+F11
(b) Alt+F8
(c) Ctrl+ Break
(d) Ctrl+ G

12] is the shortcut to stop execution of programs in VBA IDE
(a) Alt+F11
(b) Alt+F8
(c) Ctrl+ Break
(d) Ctrl+ G

13] ______ is the shortcut to display information relating to selected component in VBA IDE

(a) Ctrl+I

(b) Ctrl+J

(c) Ctrl+R

(d) Ctrl+Shift+I

14] ______is the shortcut to properties and methods of a component in VBA IDE

(a) Ctrl+ I

(b) Ctrl+ J

(c) Ctrl+ R

(d) Ctrl+ Shift+ I

15]_______ is the shortcut to display project explorer in VBA IDE

(a) Ctrl+ I

(b) Ctrl+ J

(c) Ctrl+ R

(d) Ctrl+ Shift+ I

16] ______is the shortcut to display parameter information for selected element in VBA IDE

(a) Ctrl +I

(b) Ctrl+ J

(c) Ctrl+ R

(d) Ctrl+ Shift+ I

17] _______is the shortcut to add breakpoint in VBA IDE

(a) F9

(b) F5

(c) F1

(d) F2

18] ______is the shortcut to display object browser in VBA IDE

(a) F9

(b) F5

(c) F1

(d) F2

19] _______is the shortcut to display properties window in VBA IDE

(a) F4

(b) F5

(c) F1

(d) F2

20]__________structure is useful for decision involving three or more options

a) Switch

b) Select case

c) Function

d) List

21] VBA has a coding, compilation, running and debugging environment called

(a) Integrated Development Environment (IDE)

(b) Editor

(c) Highlighter

(d) Compiler

22] In VBA, the function Asc converts given character value to numeric code in______ system

(a) American Standard Code for Information Interchange (ASCII)

(b) Double Byte Character Set (DBCS)

(c) Unicode

(d) none of them

23] In VBA, the function AscB converts given character value to numeric code in ______system]

(a) American Standard Code for Information Interchange (ASCII)

(b) Double Byte Character Set (DBCS)

(c) Unicode

(d) none of them

24] In VBA, the function AscW converts given character value to numeric code in ________system

(a) American Standard Code for Information Interchange (ASCII)

(b) Double Byte Character Set (DBCS)

(c) Unicode

(d) none of them

25] In VBA, the function Chr converts given numeric value to character value in ________system

(a) American Standard Code for Information Interchange (ASCII)

(b) Double Byte Character Set (DBCS)

(c) Unicode

(d) none of them

26] In VBA, the function ChrB converts given numeric value to character value in ______system]

(a) American Standard Code for Information Interchange (ASCII)
(b) <u>Double Byte Character Set (DBCS)</u>
(c) Unicode
(d) none of them

27] In VBA, the function ChrW converts given numeric value to character value in ________system
(a) American Standard Code for Information Interchange (ASCII)
(b) Double Byte Character Set (DBCS)
(c) <u>Unicode System</u>
(d) none of them

28] In VBA, Cstr function converts any data to______ type
(a) Integer
(b) Double
(c) Single
(d) <u>String</u>

29] CDbl function converts String to __________type
(a) Integer
(b) <u>Double</u>
(c) Single
(d) String

30] In VBA, CInt function converts String to ________type
(a) <u>Integer</u>
(b) Double
(c) Single
(d) String

31] In VBA, Csng function converts String to ________type]
(a) Integer
(b) Double
(c) <u>Single</u>
(d) String

32] In VBA, Val function converts String to ________type
(a) <u>number</u>
(b) byte
(c) Currency
(d) Decimal

33] In VBA, CByte function converts String to _______type
(a) number
(b) <u>byte</u>

(c) Currency

(d) Decimal

34] In VBA, CCur function converts String to ________type

(a) number

(b) byte

(c) Currency

(d) Decimal

35] In VBA, CLng function converts String to________ type

(a) Long

(b) byte

(c) Currency

(d) Decimal

36] In VBA, CDec function converts String to________ type

(a) number

(b) byte

(c) Currency

(d) Decimal

37] _______function in VBA creates a custom error message

(a) Format

(b) CVErr

(c) InputBox

(d) MsgBox

38] _________function in VBA formats a number according to given text strings containing 0, # and comma (,)

(a) Format

(b) CVErr

(c) InputBox

(d) MsgBox

39] Boolean data type in VBA has size of _______

(a) 1 byte

(b) 2 bytes

(c) 3 bytes

(d) 4 bytes

40] Byte data type in VBA has size of_________

(a) 1 byte

(b) 2 bytes

(c) 3 bytes

(d) 4 bytes

1] Which of the following describes e-commerce?

A] doing business electronically

B] doing business

C] sale of goods

D] all of the above

2] Which of the following is part of the four main types for e-commerce?

A] b2b

B] b2c

C] c2b

D] all of the above

3] Which segment do eBay, Amazon]com belong?

A] b2bs

B] b2cs

C] c2bs

D] c2cs

4] Which type of e-commerce focuses on consumers dealing with each other?

A] b2b

B] b2c

C] c2b

D] c2c

5] Which segment is eBay an example?

A] b2b

B] c2b

C] c2c

D] none of the above

6] Which type deals with auction?

A] b2b

B] b2c

C] c2b

D] c2c

7] In which website Global Easy Buy is facilitated?

A] ebay.com

B] amazon.com

C] yepme.com

D] none of these

8] The best products to sell in B2C e-commerce are:

A] small products

B] digital products
C] specialty products
D] fresh products

9] Which products are people most likely to be more uncomfortable buying on the Internet?
A] books
B] furniture
C] movies
D] all of the above

10] Which products are people most likely to be comfortable buying on the Internet?
A] books
B] pcs
C] cds
D] all of the above

11] Digital products are best suited for B2C e-commerce because they:
A] are commodity like products
B] can be mass-customized and personalized
C] can be delivered at the time of purchase
D] all of the above

12] The solution for all business needs is
A] edi
B] erp
C] scm
D] none of the above

13] All of the following are techniques B2C e-commerce companies use to attract customers, except:
A] registering with search engines
B] viral marketing
C] online ads
D] virtual marketing

14] Which is a function of E-commerce
A] marketing
B] advertising
C] warehousing
D] all of the above

15] Which is not a function of E-commerce
A] marketing

B] advertising

C] warehousing

D] none of the above

16] Which term represents a count of the number of people who visit one site, click on an ad, and are taken to the site of the advertiser?

A] affiliate programs

B] click-through

C] spam

D] all of the above

17] What is the percentage of customers who visit a Web site and actually buy something called?

A] affiliate programs

B] click-through

C] spam

D] conversion rate

18] What are materials used in production in a manufacturing company or are placed on the shelf for sale in a retail environment?

A] direct materials

B] indirect materials

C] edi

D] none of the above

19] What are materials that are necessary for running a modern corporation, but do not relate to the company's primary business activities?

A] direct materials

B] indirect materials

C] edi

D] none of the above

20] What are ballpoint pens purchased by a clothing company?

A] direct materials

B] indirect materials

C] edi

D] none of the above

21] What is another name for?

A] direct materials

B] indirect materials

C] edi

D] none of the above

22] What is the process in which a buyer posts its interest in buying a certain quantity of items, and sellers compete for the business by submitting successively lower bids until there is only one seller left?

A] b2b marketplace

B] intranet

C] reverse auction

D] internet

23] What are plastic cards the size of a credit card that contains an embedded chip on which digital information can be stored?

A] customer relationship management systems cards

B] e-government identity cards

C] fedi cards

D] smart cards

24] Most individuals are familiar with which form of e-commerce?

A] b2b

B] b2c

C] c2b

D] c2c

25] Which form of e-commerce currently accounts for about 97% of all e-commerce revenues?

A] b2b

B] b2c

C] c2b

D] c2c

26] Which of the following are advantages normally associated with B2B e-commerce?

A] shorter cycle times

B] reduction in costs

C] reaches wider audiences

D] all of the above

27] If the threat of substitute products or services is low it is a(n):

A] disadvantage to the supplier

B] advantage to the buyer

C] advantage to the supplier

D] none of the above

28] The threat of new entrants is high when it is:

A] hard for customers to enter the market

B] hard for competitors to enter the market

C] easy for competitors to enter the market

D] easy for customers to enter the market

29] If it is easy for competitors to enter the market, the threat of new entrants is considered:

A] high

B] low

C] more

D] less

30] An industry is less attractive for suppliers when the rivalry among existing competitors is:

A] high

B] low

C] more

D] less

31] Unique value auction is mainly applies to?

A] new products

B] second hand products

C] engineering products

D] none of the above

32] Paisapay is facilitated in

A] ebay]co.in

B] amazon.com

C] flipkart.com

D] none of the above

33] Which of the following is a useful security mechanism when considering business strategy and IT?

A] encryption

B] decryption

C] firewall

D] all the above

34] Which of the following is not related to security mechanism

A] encryption

B] decryption

C] e-cash

D] all the above

35] A product or service that customers have come to expect from an industry, which must be offered by new entrants if they wish to compete and survive, is known as a(n)?

A] switching costs

B] loyalty programs

C] entry barriers

D] affiliate programs

36] Which of the following statements accurately reflect the impact of technology?

A] technology has caused buyer power to increase

B] technology has lessened the entry barriers for many industrie

C] technology has increased the threat of substitute products and services

D] all of the above

37] A business cannot be all things to all people] Instead, a business must:

A] identify target customers

B] identify the value of products/services as perceived by customers

C] all of the above

D] none of the above

38] How the transactions occur in e-commerce?

A] using e-medias

B] using computers only

C] using mobile phones only

D] none of the above

39] Which type of products is lesser purchased using ecommerce?

A] automobiles

B] books

C] softwares

D] none

40] A business competing in a commodity like environment must focus on which of the following?

A] price

B] ease / speed of delivery

C] ease of ordering

D] all of the above

41] Which of the following refers to creating products tailored to individual customers?

A] customization

B] aggregation

C] direct materials

D] reverse auction

42] Materials used in the normal operation of a business but not related to primary business operations are called what?

A] supplies

B] direct materials

C] <u>indirect materials</u>

D] daily stuff

43] Amazon]com is well-known for which e-commerce marketing technique?

A] banner ads

B] pop-up ads

C] <u>affiliate programs</u>

D] viral marketing

44] What is the name given to an interactive business providing a centralized market where many buyers and suppliers can come together for e-commerce or commerce-related activities?

A] direct marketplace

B] b2b

C] b2c

D] <u>electronic marketplace</u>

45] Which form of e-marketplace brings together buyers and sellers from multiple industries, often for MRO materials?

A] <u>horizontal</u>

B] vertical

C] integrated

D] inclined

46] Which form of e-marketplace brings together buyers and sellers from the same industry?

A] horizontal

B] <u>vertical</u>

C] integrated

D] inclined

47] Which type of add appears on a web page?

A] pop-under ad

B] pop-up ad

C] <u>banner ad</u>

D] discount ad

48] What type of ad appears on top of a web page?

A] pop-under ad
B] pop-up ad
C] banner ad
D] discount ad

49] What type of ad appears under a web page?

A] pop-under ad
B] pop-up ad
C] banner ad
D] discount ad

50] Which, if any, of the following types of ads are people most willing to tolerate?

A] pop-under ad
B] pop-up ad
C] banner ad
D] none of the above

Q. 1 ________ is the practice and precautions taken to protect valuable information from unauthorized access, recording, disclosure or destruction.

A] Network Security
B] Database Security
C] Information Security
D] Physical Security

Q. 2 ________ platforms are used for safety and protection of information in the cloud.

A] Cloud workload protection platforms
B] Cloud security protocols
C] AWS
D] One Drive

Q. 3 Compromising confidential information comes under__

A] Bug
B] Threat
C] Vulnerability
D] Attack

Q. 4 An attempt to harm, damage or cause threat to a system or network is broadly termed as _______

A] Cyber-crime
B] Cyber Attack
C] System hijacking
D] Digital crime

Q. 5 The CIA triad is often represented by which of the following?

A] <u>Triangle</u>

B] Diagonal

C] Ellipse

D] Circle

Q. 6 Related to information security, confidentiality is the opposite of which of the following?

A] Closure

B] <u>Disclosure</u>

C] Disaster

D] Disposal

Q. 8 _______ means the protection of data from modification by unknown users.

A] Confidentiality

B] <u>Integrity</u>

C] Authentication

D] Non-repudiation

Q. 9 _______ of information means, only authorized users are capable of accessing the information.

A] Confidentiality

B] Integrity

C] Non-repudiation

D] <u>Availability</u>

Q. 10 This helps in identifying the origin of information and authentic user. This referred to here as __________

A] Confidentiality

B] Integrity

C] <u>Authenticity</u>

D] Availability

Q. 11 Data ___________ is used to ensure confidentiality.

A] <u>Encryption</u>

B] Locking

C] Decryption

D] Backup

Q. 12 What does OSI stand for in the OSI Security Architecture?

A] Open System Interface

B] <u>Open Systems Interconnections</u>

C] Open Source Initiative

D] Open Standard Interconnections

Q. 13 A company requires its users to change passwords every month. This improves the ________ of the network.

A] Performance

B] Reliability

C] Security

D] None of the above

Q. 14 Release of message contents and Traffic analysis are two types of __________ attacks.

A] Active Attack

B] Modification of Attack

C] Passive attack

D] DoS Attack

Q. 15 The ________ is encrypted text.

A] Cipher scricpt

B] Cipher text

C] Secret text

D] Secret script

Q. 17 Which of the following Algorithms not belong to symmetric encryption

A] 3DES (TripleDES)

B] RSA

C] RC5

D] IDEA

Q. 18 Which is the largest disadvantage of the symmetric Encryption?

A] More complex and therefore more time-consuming calculations.

B] Problem of the secure transmission of the Secret Key.

C] Less secure encryption function.

D] Isn't used any more.

Q. 19 In cryptography, what is cipher?

A] algorithm for performing encryption and decryption

B] encrypted message

C] both algorithm for performing encryption and decryption and encrypted message

D] decrypted message

Q. 21 Which one of the following algorithm is not used in asymmetric-key cryptography?

A] rsa algorithm

B] diffie-hellman algorithm

C] electronic code book algorithm

D] dsa algorithm

Q. 23 What is data encryption standard (DES)?

A] block cipher

B] stream cipher

C] bit cipher

D] byte cipher

Q. 24 A asymmetric-key (or public key) cipher uses

A] 1 key

B] 2 key

C] 3 key

D] 4 key

Q. 26 ________________ is the process or mechanism used for converting ordinary plain text into garbled non-human readable text & vice-versa.

A] Malware Analysis

B] Exploit writing

C] Reverse engineering

D] Cryptography

Q.27 ______________ is a means of storing & transmitting information in a specific format so that only those for whom it is planned can understand or process it.

A] Malware Analysis

B] Cryptography

C] Reverse engineering

D] Exploit writing

Q. 28 Cryptographic algorithms are based on mathematical algorithms where these algorithms use ___________ for a secure transformation of data.

A] secret key

B] external programs

C] add-ons

D] secondary key

Q. 29 Conventional cryptography is also known as _____________ or symmetric-key encryption.

A] secret-key

B] public key

C] protected key

D] primary key

Q. 30 The procedure to add bits to the last block is termed as ____________________

A] decryption

B] hashing

C] tuning

D] padding

Q. 32 ECC encryption system is ___________

A] symmetric key encryption algorithm

B] asymmetric key encryption algorithm

C] not an encryption algorithm

D] block cipher method

Q. 33 _________function creates a message digest out of a message.

A] encryption

B] decryption

C] hash

D] none of the above

Q. 34 Extensions to the X.509 certificates were added in version _____

A] 1

B] 2

C] 3

D] 4

Q. 35 A digital signature needs _____ system

A] symmetric-key

B] asymmetric-key

C] either (a) or (b)

D] neither (a) nor (b)

Q. 36 Elliptic curve cryptography follows the associative property.

A] TRUE

B] FALSE

Q. 37 ECC stands for

A] Elliptic curve cryptography

B] Enhanced curve cryptography

C] Elliptic cone cryptography

D] Eclipse curve cryptography

Q. 38 When a hash function is used to provide message authentication, the hash function value is referred to as

A] Message Field

B] Message Digest

C] Message Score

D] Message Leap

Q. 39 Message authentication code is also known as

A] key code

B] hash code

C] keyed hash function

Q. 40 The main difference in MACs and digital signatures is that, in digital signatures the hash value of the message is encrypted with a user's public key.

A] TRUE

B] FALSE

Q. 41 The DSS signature uses which hash algorithm?

A] MD5

B] SHA-2

C] SHA-1

D] Does not use hash algorithm

Q. 42 What is the size of the RSA signature hash after the MD5 and SHA-1 processing?

A] 42 bytes

B] 32 bytes

C] 36 bytes

D] 48 bytes

Q. 43 In the handshake protocol which is the message type first sent between client and server ?

A] server_hello

B] client_hello

C] hello_request

D] certificate_request

Q. 44 One commonly used public-key cryptography method is the _______ algorithm.

A] RSS

B] RAS

C] RSA

D] RAA

Q. 45 The _________ method provides a one-time session key for two parties.

A] Diffie-Hellman

B] RSA

C] DES

D] AES

Q. 46 The __________ attack can endanger the security of the Diffie-Hellman method if two parties are not authenticated to each other.

A] man-in-the-middle

B] ciphertext attack

C] plaintext attack

D] none of the above

Q. 48 VPN is abbreviated as __________

A] Visual Private Network

B] Virtual Protocol Network

C] Virtual Private Network

D] Virtual Protocol Networking

Q. 49 __________ provides an isolated tunnel across a public network for sending and receiving data privately as if the computing devices were directly connected to the private network.

A] Visual Private Network

B] Virtual Protocol Network

C] Virtual Protocol Networking

D] Virtual Private Network

Q. 50 Which of the statements are not true to classify VPN systems?

A] Protocols used for tunnelling the traffic

B] Whether VPNs are providing site-to-site or remote access connection

C] Securing the network from bots and malwares

D] Levels of security provided for sending and receiving data privately

Engineering Chemistry MCQ for Computer Engineering

1. Valence Bond Theory was developed in the year

a) 1916

b) 1927

c) 1930

d) 1932

2. According to VBT, the formation of a stable bond requires

a) The electrons should have opposite spins

b) The two atoms should be close to each other

c) The greater overlapping of the electron clouds

d) All of the mentioned

3. The s-orbital does not show preference to any direction because

a) It is the smallest orbital

b) It is present in every atom

c) It is spherically symmetric

d) It is the first orbital

4. The p-orbital is in the shape of a

a) Sphere

b) Dumbbell

c) Pear-shaped lobe

d) None of the mentioned

6. According to VBT, the direction of a bond which is formed due to overlapping will be

a) In the same direction in which orbitals are concentrated

b) In the opposite direction in which orbitals are concentrated

c) Perpendicular to the direction in which orbitals are concentrated

d) None of the mentioned

7. Which orbital would form more stronger bond if both of them have identical stability?

a) The one which is less directionally concentrated

b) The one which is more directionally concentrated

c) Both will be equally strong

d) It differs from atom to atom

8. The different types of energies associated with a molecule are

a) Electronic energy

b) Vibrational energy

c) Rotational energy

d) All of the mentioned

9. During the motion, if the centre of gravity of molecule changes, the molecule possess

a) Electronic energy

b) Rotational energy

c) Translational energy

d) Vibrational energy

10. The correct order of different types of energies is

a) Eel >> Evib >> Erot >> E tr

b) Eel >> Erot >> Evib >> E tr

c) Eel >> Evib >> Etr >> E rot

d) Etr >> Evib >> Erot >> E el

11. The region of electromagnetic spectrum for nuclear magnetic resonance is

a) Microwave

b) Radio frequency

c) Infrared

d) UV-rays

12. Which of the following is an application of molecular spectroscopy?

a) Structural investigation

b) Basis of understanding of colors

c) Study of energetically excited reaction products

d) All of the mentioned

13. Select the correct statement from the following option.

a) Spectroscopic methods require less time and more amount of sample than classical methods

b) Spectroscopic methods require more time and more amount of sample than classical methods

c) Spectroscopic methods require less time and less amount of sample than classical methods

d) Spectroscopic methods require more time and less amount of sample than classical methods

14. The transition zone for Raman spectra is

a) Between vibrational and rotational levels

b) Between electronic levels

c) Between magnetic levels of nuclei

d) Between magnetic levels of unpaired electrons

15. The criteria for electronic spin resonance is

a) Periodic change in polarisability

b) Spin quantum number of nuclei > 0

c) Presence of unpaired electron in a molecule

d) Presence of chromophore in a molecule

Engineering Physics MCQ for Computer Engineering

1. Which one of the following is the property of an ionic compound?

a) High melting and boiling points

b) Low melting and boiling points

c) Weak inter-atomic forces

d) Non conductors of electricity

2. When do ionic compounds conduct electricity?

a) In gaseous state

b) In solid state

c) When dissolved in water

d) They never conduct

3. Which of the following covalent compounds conduct electricity?

a) Silica

b) Graphite

c) Diamond

d) Hydrogen chloride

4. Which of the following is a crystalline solid?

a) Anisotropic substances

b) Isotropic substances

c) Supercooled liquids

d) Amorphous solids

5. Why are the glasses of building milky?

a) Because of unwanted deposits

b) Because it becomes old

c) Because it is brittle

d) Because it changes in properties

6. Which of the following has body centered cubic structure?

a) Polonium

b) Copper

c) Nickel

d) Tungsten

7. What is the possible number of different types of lattices (3D)?

a) 4

b) 8

c) 14

d) 17

8. What is the lattice constant for FCC crystal having atomic radius 1.476 Å

a) 1.476 Å

b) 4.1748 Å

c) 5.216 Å

d) 0

9. The interplanar spacing of (220) planes of a FCC structure is 1.7458 Å. Calculate the lattice constant.

a) 4.983 Å

b) 2.458 Å

c) 0

d) 5.125 Å

10. Iron has a BCC structure with atomic radius 0.123 Å. Find the lattice constant.

a) 0

b) 4.587 Å

c) 2.314 Å

d) <u>0.2840 Å</u>

11. Which of the following is true about the universe?

a) It is an open system

b) It is a closed system

c) <u>It is an isolated system</u>

d) It is an international system

12. Which of the following holds good in all natural processes?

a) The Doppler Effect

b) <u>Newton's law of gravitation</u>

c) Electromagnetic law

d) Lenz's law

13. Which of the following leads to the law of conservation of energy?

a) Gravity

b) Isotropy

c) Nuclear force

d) <u>Homogeneity of time</u>

14. Which of the following leads to the law of conservation of angular momentum?

a) <u>Isotropy of space</u>

b) Homogeneity of time

c) Nuclear force

d) Gravity

15. Which of the following is the SI unit of luminous intensity?

a) Sterdian

b) Radian

c) Mole

d) <u>Candela</u>

16. Sterdian is the SI unit of which of the following?

a) Phase angle

b) Luminous intensity

c) Mass

d) Solid angle

17. How many light years are there in one metre?

a) 9.46×1015ly

b) 1.057×10-16ly

c) 1ly

d) 1×10-16ly

18. The radius of gold nucleus is 41.3fermi. Express its volume in m3.

a) 41.3×10-15 m3

b) 2.95×10-40 m3

c) 4.19 m3

d) 29.33 m3

19. Convert an acceleration of 2km/h2 into cm/s2.

a) 2×105 cm/s2

b) 0.0027 cm/s2

c) 0.0154 cm/s2

d) 0.055 cm/s2

Environmental Science for Computer Engineering

1. The average quantity of water (in lpcd) required for domestic purposes according to IS code is _________

a) 100

b) 120

c) 70

d) 135

2. The average consumption of water required in factories in lpcd is _____________

a) 10-15

b) 20-30

c) 30-45

d) 70-80

3. In which type of water demand, minimum average consumption of water takes place?

a) Domestic water demand

b) Industrial water demand

c) Institutional and commercial water demand

d) Fire demand

4. What is the minimum water pressure available at fire hydrants?

a) 80-100kN/m^2

b) 100-150kN/m^2

c) 40-60kN/m²

d) 150-200kN/m²

6. What is the fire demand of the city of 1lakh population by Buston's formula?

a) 5663

b) 56630

c) 566300

d) 5663000

7. Water lost in theft and waste contributes to how much % of total consumption?

a) 5

b) 10

c) 15

d) 20

8. Which is the correct statement regarding per capita demand?

a) Daily water required by an individual

b) Water required for various purposes by a person

c) Water required by an individual in a year

d) Annual average amount of daily water required by one person

9. What are the factors affecting per capita demand?

a) Size of city

b) Size of city, habit of people

c) Cost of water, quality of water, size of city

d) Cost of water, quality of water, size of city, habit of people

10. Which of the following statement is correct?

a) Rich class consumes less water

b) Intermittent water supplies leads to less water consumption

c) Loss of water is more if the pressure in the distribution system is less

d) Water consumption is less in flush system

11. If the annual average hourly demand of the city is 10000m3, what is the maximum hourly consumption?

a) 2700 m3

b) 27000 m3

c) 270000 m

d) 2700000 m3

12. If in a city, the maximum daily draft is 25MLD, fire draft is 35MLD and maximum hourly draft is 40MLD, what is the coincident draft?

a) 60MLD

b) 40MLD
c) 25MLD
d) 35MLD
13. What is the design period for the water treatment unit?
a) 10 years
b) 15 years
c) 20 years
d) 30 years
14. What is the design discharge for intake structures?
a) Maximum daily demand
b) Maximum hourly demand
c) Maximum weekly demand
d) Average daily demand
15. In which of the following units, design period is maximized?
a) Distribution system
b) Demand reservoir
c) Water treatment unit
d) Pipe mains
16. Suspended solids are measured by which of the following?
a) Turbidity rod
b) Gravimetric test
c) Chromatography
d) Jackson's turbidity meter
17. The maximum permissible limit for suspended solids is ___
a) 10 mg/l
b) 20 mg/l
c) 30 mg/l
d) 40 mg/l
18. Identify the correct relation between the following?
a) Dissolved solid = Total solid + Suspended solid
b) Dissolved solid = Total solid – Suspended solid
c) Total solid = Dissolved solid / Suspended solid
d) Dissolved solid = Suspended solid – Total solid
19. Which method is used to measure the color of water?
a) Gravimetric analysis
b) Chromatography
c) Tintometer method
d) Hydrometer analysis

20. 1 TCU (True Color Unit) is equivalent to ______
a) The color produced by 1 g of platinum cobalt
b) The color produced by 1 mg of platinum cobalt
c) The color produced by 1 mg of platinum cobalt in 1L of distilled water
d) The color produced by 1 mg of platinum cobalt in 1mL of distilled water

21. The range for threshold odour number is
a) 0-3
b) 1-5
c) 1-3
d) 0-5

22. One JTU is equivalent to turbidity produced by
a) 1mg of fine silica dissolved in 1L of distilled water
b) 1g of fine silica dissolved in 1L of distilled water
c) 1g of fine silica dissolved in 1ml of distilled water
d) 1mg of fine silica dissolved in 1ml of distilled water

23. If the PO value is 6, what does it imply?
a) No perceptible odour
b) Very faint odour
c) Very distinct odour
d) Extremely strong odour

24. The range of temperature of water that is required to do the temperature test is__ 0C.
a) 10-25
b) 0-25
c) 10-30
d) 20-30

25. Which of the following statement is wrong regarding turbidity?
a) It is an extent to which light is absorbed by particles in the water
b) It is expressed in ppm
c) It depends on the fineness of particle present in the water
d) Turbidity rod is a laboratory method to measure turbidity

26. The permissible limit of turbidity of domestic water is _____ ppm.
a) 5-10
b) 1-5
c) 10-50
d) 10-30

27. What is the full form of NTU in context with turbidity?

a) Number of transfer unit

b) Neurological turbidity unit

c) Nephelometric turbidity unit

d) Network terminal unit

28. When depth of insertion of turbidity rod increases, the reading in the turbidity rod ___

a) Decreases

b) Increases

c) First decrease, then increase

d) Remains constant

Electrical & Electronics MCQ for Computer Engineering

85] A heater draws a current of 8A when connected to a 240V source] What is the resistance value of the heater element in ohms?

A] 40

B] 20

C] 30

D] 60

86] An electric soldering iron with an 80 ohms heating element is plugged into a 240V outlet] How much current will be drawn by the iron?

A] 2A

B] 3A

C] 4A

D] 5A

87] The alternator in a car delivers 4A and has a load of 3 ohms connected across its terminals] Find the voltage of the circuit

A] 18V

B] 24V

C] 12V

D] 16V

88] Three resistors of 1K ohms, 2K ohms and 7K ohms are connected in series with a 30 V supply] If 2 K ohms and 7 K ohms resistors are open circuited, a voltmeter connected across the 7K ohms resistor will indicate...

A] 10 k ohms, 3A

B] 10 k ohms, 300mA

C] 10 k ohms, 3 mA

D] 5 k ohms, 6 mA

89] A voltage source produces an IR drop of 40V across a 20 ohms resistance, 60V across a 30 ohms resistance and 180V across a 90 ohms resistance all in series] How much is the applied voltage?

A] 180 V

B] 240 V

C] 100 V

D] <u>280 V</u>

90] Three resistors 27 ohms, 47 ohms and 68 ohms are connected in parallel] What is the otal resistance?

A] <u>less than 27 ohms</u>

B] greater than 68 ohms

C] between 27 and 47 ohms

D] sum of all the three resistances

91] One million and one mege ohms resistors are there if connected both in parallel, what would be the combined resistance value?

A] <u>0.5 mega ohm</u>

B] 0.5 milli ohm

C] 0.5 kilo ohm

D] 0.5 ohm

92] A 24 ohms and a 8 ohms resistors in parallel gets a combined resistance of...

A] <u>6 ohms</u>

B] 12 ohms

C] 3 ohms

D] 32 ohms

93] Resistors of the following values are connected in parallel, 5 ohms, 5 kilo-ohms, 50 kilo-ohms, 5 mega ohms] Their equivalent resistance will be very near to...

A] <u>4.5 ohms</u>

B] 4500 ohms

C] 45000 ohms

D] 4,500,000 ohms

94] The resistance of given wire is 2 ohms] The resistance of the other wire made of the same material having twice the length and twice the cross sectional area is...

A] 5 ohms

B] 6 ohms

C] <u>2 ohms</u>

D] 8 ohms

95] If the area of a metal wire of a given length is doubles, its resistance will...

A] be doubled

B] be halved

C] remain the same

D] be four times more

96].Among the following only one is regarded as resistance wire

A] gold

B] silver

C] nichrome

D] copper

97] Arc heating occurs when the air between electrodes of opposite polarity becomes..

A] moistened

B] dry

C] ionized

D] none of the above

98] The meter used to measure the temperature of furnace is...

A] hydrometer

B] pyrometer

C] hygrometer

D] tachometer

99] in the case of electrolyte a rise in temperature causes...

A] decrease in resistance

B] increase in resistance

C] no change in resistance

D] none of the above

100] Heat developed in a conductor is proportional to the...

A] square of the power

B] square of the resistance

C] square of the current

D] square of the time

101] Out of the four metal/alloys given below, one has almost no change in resistance for temperature change...

A] nickel

B] nichrome

C] platinum

D] manganin

102] A material that is slightly repelled by a magnet is called ...
A] magnetic
B] paramagnetic
C] diamagnetic
D] ferromagnetic

103] A material that can be magnetized only very slightly is called...
A] magnetic
B] paramagnetic
C] diamagnetic
D] ferromagnetic

104] Substances that can be magnetized easily and make very strong magnets are called...
A] ferromagnetic
B] diamagnetic
C] paramagnetic
D] permanent magnetic

105] A substance that has a high retentivity can be used for the manufacture of...
A] electromagnets
B] permanent magnets
C] temporary magnets
D] paramagnets

106] A substance that has low retentivity can be used for the manufacture of...
A] electromagnets
B] permanent magnets
C] bar magnets
D] paramagnets

107] The symbol for inductance is...
A] H
B] I
C] L
D] X

108] Tube lamp choke is the best example of...
A] open circuited
B] short circuited
C] grounded
D] connected to the neutral line

109] The initial function of a choke in a tube light circuit is to...

A] limit the starting current

B] induce high voltage

C] heat up the filament

D] limit the current after starting

110] The second function of a choke in a tube light circuit is to...

A] limit the starting current

B] induce high voltage

C] heat up the filament

D] limit the current after starting

111] The periodic time of a wave from is 2ms] Calculate the frequency

A] 50 HZ

B] 5 HZ

C] 500HZ

D] 5 KHZ

112] How big is the peak amplitude of a sine-wave with an effective value of 220 volts?

A] 311 V

B] 380 V

C] 400 V

D] 440 V

113] The peak-to-peak voltage is 99V] how big is the effective value of the sine wave?

A] 70 V

B] 44.5V

C] 49.5 V

D] 35 V

114] A moving coil voltmeter reads 10 V AC] How big is the effective voltage?

A] higher

B] lower

C] the same

D] 10% higher

115] A moving iron ammeter reads 10 A] how big is the peak current of the oscillation?

A] 7.07 A

B] 1.1414A

C] 70.7 A

D] <u>14.1 A</u>

116] A current of 2 amps flows through a resistance of 10 ohms] The power dissipated in the resistance is equal to...

A] 20 watts

B] 200 watts

C] <u>40 watts</u>

D] 5 watts

117] If the frequency changes from 50 HZ to 100 HZ keeping voltage constant, the inductive reactance of coil connected to supply...

A] remains same

B] become half

C] <u>become doubled</u>

D] become 4 times

118] Capacitance is not affected by...

A] plate area

B] distance between plates

C] dialectic material

D] <u>frequency</u>

119] The capacitive reactance of a capacitor varies...

A] directly with frequency

B] <u>inversely with frequency</u>

C] directly with applied voltage

D] inversely with applied voltage

120] A capacitor acquired 3 coulombs of charge when 6 volts are applied across it] It has a capacitance of ...

A] <u>0.5 farad</u>

B] 3 farads

C] 3 farads

D] 18 farads

121] A capacitor is connected across a 200 volt AC line, its minimum voltage rating should be...

A] 100 volts

B] 200 Volts

C] <u>300 volts</u>

D] 400 volts

122] when testing a capacitor with an ohmmeter, the meter indicates some resistance] The capacitor under test is...

A] <u>leaky</u>

B] open

C] good

D] short

123] The total capacitance of a 40 micro farad capacitor connected in series with an 80 micro farad capacitor is...

A] 26.7 micro farad

B] 40 micro farad

C] 60.6 micro farad

D] 120 micro farad

124] For obtaining 1 micro farad capacitor from 3 nos] of 3 micro farad capacitors we have to connect...

A] all in parallel

B] all in series

C] 2 series and one in parallel

D] none of the above

125] In an AC series circuit having R and C the current flowing through the capacitor will be...

A] lagging the voltage

B] leading the voltage

C] in phase with the voltage

D] none of the above

126] If the frequency of the supply is increased in the R-C series circuit the capacitive reactance will be

A] reduced

B] increased

C] having no effect

D] none of the above

127] Power companies are interested in improving the power factor to

A] reduce line current

B] increase motor efficiency

C] increase volt-amperes

D] decrease power

128] A capacitor increases the power factor value of an AC motor load when it is connected...

A] in series with the motor

B] in series with the starter

C] in parallel with the motor

D] in series with the main winding

129] Normally, the power factor of an incandescent lighting circuit is..

A] 0

B] 0.5

C] 0.707

D] 1.0

130] When resistance alone is used to determine current in an RLC series circuit, the circuit is...

A] an inductive circuit

B] a capacitive circuit

C] a combination circuit

D] a resonant circuit

131] Inductive reactance is directly related to..

A] resistance

B] frequency

C] capacitance

D] power

132] Synchronous motor when used for power factor improvement should be...

A] under excited

B] over excited

C] loaded

D] running at no load

133] In a RL parallel circuit, the opposition to total current is called...

A] reactance

B] resistance

C] a vector sum

D] impedance

134] In a AC parallel RL circuit, the power dissipated at the

A] impedance

B] resistance

C] inductance

D] capacitance

135] How much is the nominal output voltage of a carbon zinc cell?

A] 12V

B] 1.5V

C] 2.0V

D] 2.2V

136] Cells are connected in series to..

A] increase the output voltage

B] decreases the output voltage

C] decrease the internal resistance

D] increase the current capacity

54137connected in

A] series

B] parallel

C] series-parallel

D] parallel-series

138] The capacity of a cell is measured in

A] watt-hour

B] watts

C] amperes

D] ampere-hour

139] The primary cell which has the shortest shelf life is

A] carbon – zinc

B] alkaline

C] mercury

D] lithium

140] The cell which has very high energy density for given weight or volume to

A] carbon-zinc

B] alkaline

C] mercury

D] lithium

141] A 100-Ah capacity battery should deliver a current of 8A for approximately...

A] 12 h

B] 8 h

C] 20 h

D] 100 h

142] When the battery is needed to be kept idle for a long time...

A] overcharge the battery

B] remove electrolyte

C] clean the plates with distilled water

D] dry them and store the battery in cool dry clean place

143] The active materials of the nickel iron cell are...

A] nickel hydroxide

B] powdered iron and its oxide
C] 21% solution of caustic potash
D] all the above materials
144] The capacity of a cell is measured in
A] watt hour
B] watts
C] amperes
D] ampere-hour
145] To charge a secondary cell, the system used is
A] low voltage AC
B] high voltage AC
C] AC
D] DC
146] What is the number of phases in a normal industrial supply system?
A] one
B] three
C] four
D] two
147] In a 3 phase star connected alternator, the coils have a phase difference of...
A] 120◦
B] 240◦
C] 60◦
D] 360◦
148] Delta connection is used no one of the following
A] primary of the transmission line transformer
B] alternator winding
C] secondary of the distribution transformer
D] primary of the distribution transformer
149] Which method can be used to measure the power in a 3-phase unbalanced load system?
A] one wattmeter method
B] tow wattmeter method
C] three wattmeter method
D] three ammeter method
150] Two wattmeters can be used to measure 3-hase power in a 3-phase, 3 wire system with...
A] balanced load

B] unbalanced load

C] balanced as well as unbalanced load

D] out of balanced load

151] A single wattmeter can be used to measure power in a 3-phase system only when the load is..

A] balanaced

B] unbalanced

C] balanced as well as unbalanced load

D] constant

152] The force producing movement of the pointer in an indicating instrument is called as...

A] deflecting force

B] controlling force

C] damping force

D] distracting force

153] A permanent magnet moving coil instrument will read...

A] only AC quantities

B] only DC quantities

C] both AC and DC quantities

D] pulsating quantities

154] An instrument using gravity control will read correctly if used in..

A] vertical position only

B] horizontal position only

C] inclined position only

D] any position

155] Which one of the following damping methods is used in permanent magnet moving coil instrument?

A] air damping

B] fluid damping

C] spring damping

D] eddy current damping

156] Moving coil instrument works on the effect of...

A] chemical effect

B] heating effect

C] electrostatic effect

D] electromagnetic effect

157] The meter installed at your house to measure electrical energy is an example of...

A] indication type instrument

B] recording type instrument

C] indicating as well as recording type instrument

D] integrating type instrument

158].Which of the following material is preferred for permanent magnet?

A] alnico

B] y-alloy

C] silicon steel

D] wrought iron

159] The instrument which could be classified as absolute instrument is...

A] milli ammeter

B] micro ammeter

C] galvanometer

D] tangent galvanomer

160] Which of the following methods of damping is commonly used in moving iron instrument?

A] Air damping

B] fluid damping

C] eddy current damping

D] viscosity damping

161] The deflecting torque of a moving iron instrument is directly proportional to the..

A] current

B] square of the current

C] square root of the current

D] voltage

162]Which of the following is used for measuring the medium resistance directly?

A] ammeter

B] megger

C] ohmmeter

D] voltmeter

163] An ohmmeter is used for measuring the...

A] insulation resistance

B] resistance

C] current

D] potential difference

164] Which of the following components is not a part of an ohmmeter?

A] fixed resistor

B] variable resistor

C] capacitor

D] battery

165] In shunt ohmmeter, maximum deflection signifies ..

A] maximum resistance

B] minimum resistance

C] a fault in the megger

D] none of these

166].An unknown DC voltage is to be measured, which measuring range will you select first?

A] 500V

B] 50V

C] 1.5 V

D] 0.5V

167].An unknown direct current of micro ampere rating is to be measured, which measuring range will you select first?

A] 20 micro amp

B] 15 micro amp

C] 150 micro amp

D] 500 micro amp

168] A multimeter cannot measure...

A] current

B] potential difference

C] capacitance

D] resistance

169] Dynamometer type meters are used to measure...

A] only AC quantities

B] only DC quantities

C] both AC and DC

D] pulsating AC only

170] Which effect is used in wattmeter?

A] electrodynamic effect

B] thermal effect

C] chemical effect

D] electrostatic effect

171] Which of the instrument listed below operates efficiently as wattmeter in both AC and DC?

A] PMMC instrument

B] dynamometer instrument

C] hot wire instrument

D] MI instrument

172] Electrodynamic type of instrument are used commonly for the measurement of...

A] voltage

B] current

C] resistance D]

173] When the phase and neutral of the energy meter are interchanged, its disc...

A] rotates in reverse direction

B] rotates in correct direction

C] will stop

D] rotates slowly

E] rotates at high speed

174] When the disc of energy meter is rotating even without connecting any load, the error is called

A] creeping error

B] phase error

C] friction error

D] temperature error

175] AC single phase energy meters record the energy in the unit of...

A] kilowatt hours

B] number of thousands of disc rotation

C] volt amperes

D] kilo volt ampere

176] A megger measures resistance in...

A] ohms

B] hundreds of ohms

C] thousands of ohms

D] millions of ohms

177] A megger is exclusively designed for measuring..

A] very high resistance

B] very low resistance

C] ground faults in power lines

D] over loads on DC motors

178] For pipe earthing the minimum internal diameter of galvanized iron of steel pipe required is...

A] 12.5 mm

B] 16mm

C] 3.5 mm

D] 4 m

179] The earth conductor provides a path to ground for..

A] leakage current

B] over current

C] high voltage

D] circuit current

180] if the size of the circuit copper conductor is 10 sq-mm then the size of earth conductor in G.I] wire should be...

A] 1.5 sq.mm

B] 2.5 sq.mm

C] 5 sq.mm

D] 10 sq.mm

181] One calory is equal to,,,

A] 4187 joules

B] 418.7 joules

C] 41.87 joules

D] 4.187 joules

182] The operating temperature range of electrical stove with bare heating element is...

A] 300° to 400°C

B] 500° to 600°C

C] 550° to 900°C

D] 1100° to 1300°C

183] Which appliance works on heating effect of electric current?

A] incandescent lamp

B] bimetallic thermostat

C] H R C fuse

D] toaster

184] What is the size of nichrome wire for heating element of 1000 watts, 230V heater at 500°C?

A] 18 SWG

B] 20SWG

C] 24 SWG

D] 25 SWG

185] The heat proof insulating material used for heater base is...

A] mica

B] porcelain

C] asbestos

D] glass wool

186].The temperature regulating component of an automatic electric iron is...

A] heating element

B] thermostat

C] sole plate

D] pressure plate

187].The bread toasting zone temperature is about...

A] 400◦C

B] 800◦C

C] 260◦C

D] 975◦C

188] If a winding makes electrical contact with the metal case of the mixer motor the winding is...

A] grounded

B] open circuited

C] short circuited

D] loose connected

189] If the end shafts of a rotor turns blue it is an indication of...

A] scoring

B] overheating

C] freezing

D] burring

190] What type of motor is used in a food mixer?

A] DC shunt motor

B] universal motor

C] capacitor start motor

D] capacitor start and run motor

191] In what position is the motor mounted in most of the mixers?

A] vertical

B] horizontal

C] inclined
D] parallel

INDUSTRIAL TRAINING INSTITUTE

Monthly Test-1, Marks- 20, Date:- ______________

(Every Question Carry Two Marks)

1] ABC stands for --------------
A] Automatic Breathing Control
B] Automatic Blood Control
C] Airway Breathing Circulation
D] Automatic Blood Circulation
3] To put off"Class B" fire, the types of fire extinguisher used is ....
A] dry power
B] Carbon dioxide
C] Jet of water
D] Foam type
4] Which type of fire extinguisher is used to put off general fire?
A] Water type Extinguisher
B] Foam type Extinguisher
C] Dry chemical powder Extinguisher
D] Carbon dioxide (C02] Extinguisher
5] In case of bleeding, take treatment Of
D] cold 3" and rest
A] spray cold water
B] Bandage immediately -----.
B] Enquire about the accident thought treatment
6] in case of an accident, the victim should im
A] Asked to take rest
C] Attended immediately
D] leave him
7] First aid is given to an injured or ill person primarily....
A] Save life
B] Prevent further deterioration of the muff's
C] Give best possible comfort
D] All of these
Q.1. Which of the following is the biggest unit of memory?
A] Gigabytes.
B] bytes.
C] Megabytes.

D] Kilobytes.

Q.2. The primary purpose of software is to turn data into.

A] Website.

B] Infromation.

C] Programs.

D] Objects.

Q.3. GUI Stands for

A] Graphical User Interface.

B] Greater User Interface.

C] Graphical Union Interface.

D] Graphical User Intereat.

Q.4. Key board keys that have arrows on them are called -

A] Function Keys.

B] Navigation Keys.

C] Typewriter Keys.

D] Special purpose keys.

INDUSTRIAL TRAINING INSTITUTE

Monthly Test-2, Marks- 20, Date:- _______________

(Every Question Carry Two Marks)

Q.12. .... can be used to create and format large and complex text documents.

A] "Calculator"

B] "WordPad"

C] "Notepad"

D] "Text Pad"

Q.14. A folder system is also called a "................"

A] "Direction System"

B] "Directory System"

C] "Directory list"

D] "Folder book"

Q.17. A .... is like a container in which you can store files.

A] "Icon"

B] "document"

C] "Folder"

D] "Sheet"

Q.18. The operating system's job is .... to

A] Execute many useful commands easily.

B] to make request for service through a defined application programme interface.

C] to control the computer at the most fundamental level.

D] None of these.

Q.19. The windows interface is based on ....

A] "Graphical user Interface" or GUI

B] Application Programme Interface or] API.

C] "Clipboard"

D] None of these

Q.23. A file created using Notepad is stored with the extension..................
.

A] ".txt"

B] ".docx"

C] ".png"

D] ".jpg"

Q.25. When your computer is booted and is ready to use, the screen you see is called the ....

A] "Table top"

B] "Desktop"

C] "Laptop"

D] None of these

Q.27. .... is designed to prevent and remove spy ware.

A] User Account Control

B] Windows Firewall

C] Windows Defender

D] Parental Controls

Q.29. What is "Windows Aero"

A] It is the graphical user interface for Windows XP.

B] It is the graphical user interface for Windows Vista.

C] Application Program

D] None of these

Q.30. Which is the basic program of a computer?

A] Operating System

B] Software Program

C] Application Program

D] None of these

INDUSTRIAL TRAINING INSTITUTE

Monthly Test-3, Marks- 20, Date:- _______________

(Every Question Carry Two Marks)

Q.34. The .... Menu is used to enhance the appearance of the contained presented in a document.

A] "Insert"

B] "Edit" ?

C] "Format"

D] "File"

Q.36. "............." helps in guarding your computer against malicious software.

A] "Windows Firewall"

B] "Windows Defender"

C] "Spy ware"

D] of these.

Q.37. .... is a basic text editing programme and it is most commonly used to view or edit text files.

A] "Calculator"

B] "Notepad"

C] "Address book"

D] "Paint"

Q.38. In a windows operating system screen saver

A] is helps in guarding your computer against many types of malicious software.

B] is a long, vertical bar that is displayed on the side of your desktop.

C] is a programme that displays on image, animation, or just a blank screen on a Computer after on input has been received for a certain length of time.

D] None of these.

Q.40. The programmes on the .... in Windows Vista remain there and are always available for you to click to start them.

A] the "Most frequently use programmes list.

B] "pinned items list"

C] "Documents"

D] "Control Panel"

Q.41. In Windows Vista .... is a power-saving state.

A] Log off

B] Sleep

C] Restart

D] Lock

Q.42. AERO is an abbreviation of ....

A] Authentic, Energetic, Reflective and Open.

B] Essential, Reflective and Open.

C] Arithmetic, Essential, Reflective and Object.

D] Authentic, Essential, Reflective and Open.

Q.43. At the bottom of the screen, you can see a long, thin bar which is called as ....

A] "Task bar"

B] "Title bar"

C] "Menu bar"

D] "Spacebar"

Q.44. In Windows Vista a "Clipboard" is ....

A] an application program

B] a temporary storage area for information that you have copied or moved from one place and plan to use somewhere else.

C] an operating system.

D] None of these.

Q.45. .... is a basic text editing programme and it is most commonly used to view or edit text files.

A] "Calculator"

B] "Notepad"

C] "Address book"

D] "Paint"

INDUSTRIAL TRAINING INSTITUTE

Monthly Test-4, Marks- 20, Date:- _______________

(Every Question Carry Two Marks)

Q.46. ...., is a drawing programme that can be used to create modify graphic images.

A] "Brush"

B] "Paint"

C] "Notepad"

D] "WordPad"

Q.5. All of the following Ribbon tabs are displayed in Word 2007, EXCEPT

A] Home

B] Insert

C] Tools

D] Page Layout

Q.9. In Word, a file is called as a ....

A] "template"

B] "form"

C] "database"

D] "Document"

Q.13. A .... is a reference from one part of a document to related information in same another part.

A] Hyperlink

B] Cross-reference

C] Document

D] Linkage

Q.14. For Indentation you may use the "Decrease Indent" and "Increase Indent" icons in the "Paragraph" group on the "............" tab for indenting your text.

A] Insert

B] Home

C] Page Layout

D] Data

Q.16. The "..............." is a dictionary of synonyms which you can use to find words that are synonyms with a term.

A] Translate

B] Spelling

C] Thesaurus

D] Research

Q.17. A " .... " is a listing of the topics that appear in a document with their associated page references.

A] Index

B] Table

C] Clipboard

D] Table of contents

Q.19. A "............" is a connection to a location in the current document to another document or Web Site.

A] Link

B] hyperlink

C] hypolink

D] linkage

Q.26. A "................" is a pre-designed document useful for creating common purpose documents such as a fax, invoice or business letter.

A] Template

B] File

C] Form

D] Database

Q.28. A "............" is used to organize information into an easy-to-read format of horizontal rows and vertical columns.

A] Cell

B] Sheet

C] Box

D] Table

INDUSTRIAL TRAINING INSTITUTE

Monthly Test-5, Marks- 20, Date:- ______________

(Every Question Carry Two Marks)

Q.29. To remove individual character at the left you may press "...........".

A] Delete

B] Backspace

C] Enter

D] Spacebar

Q.30. When you click on "Format Printer" icon on the "Home" tab, you can see that your mouse pointer changes to a "............" icon.

A] paintbrush

B] I-beam

C] Arrow

D] 4-Way arrow

Q.33. When you move your mouse over a button, a .... is displayed. That provides a detailed description of what the button does.

A] Super-tooltip

B] Sub-tooltip

C] Info

D] Key-tip

Q.35. .... Applications help you to create different types of written documents such as personal letters, from letters, brochures, faxes and even professional manuals.

A] Word Processor

B] Word Pad

C] Note Pad

D] None of these

Q.40. To automatically correct the document, we use

A] The auto correct feature
B] The auto complete feature
C] Formatting
D] Building Blocks

Q.41. A "..............." is a common application for news paper columns.
A] News reading
B] News letter
C] News
D] News editor

Q.47. A "............." is used to mark a certain location in a document.
A] Index
B] Hyperlink
C] Bookmark
D] Table

Q.50. While changing the level of an item in hierarchy you can increase the indent by using
A] "Tab"
B] "Backspace"
C] "Delete"
D] "Spacebar"

Q.51. Footnotes or Endnotes are used to provide certain "..........................".
A] References
B] Information
C] Points
D] Lists

Q.1. In formula bar, an adjacent range is specified by giving the starting and editing cell addresses separated by a
A] Semicolon
B] Comma
C] Full stop
D] Colon

INDUSTRIAL TRAINING INSTITUTE

Monthly Test-6, Marks- 20, Date:- _______________

(Every Question Carry Two Marks)

Q.3. A .... is a visual representation of data and conveys the information in an easy to understand and attractive manner.
A] chart
B] table

C] picture

D] graphic

Q.4. In formulas, a non-adjacent range is specified by giving the cell addresses separated by a ....

A] Semicolon

B] Comma

C] Full stop

D] Colon

Q.20. A "..............." is a prewritten formula the performs calculations automatically.

A] "Function"

B] "Equation"

C] "Template"

D] "Reaction"

Q.21. MS Excel 2007 is used for different types of .... varying from vary simple to complex.

A] calculations

B] manipulations

C] presentations

D] expressions

Q.25. While changing the level of an item in the hierarchy you can increase the indent by using.

A] "Tab"

B] "Backspace"

C] "Delete"

D] "Spacebar"

Q.27. To remove individual character at the left you may press "..............".

A] Delete

B] Backspace

C] Enter

D] Spacebar

Q.29. The intersection of a row and a column is called a "................".

A] Table

B] Cell

C] Data

D] Sheet

Q.30. A .... is a file that is provided by the application in a "ready to use" format.

A] Sheet
B] Template
C] Book
D] Report

Q.31. A .... is a visual representation of data and conveys the information in a easy to understand and attractive manner.

A] Chart
B] Table
C] Picture
D] Graphic

Q.35. "............" are individual designs that can be applied to different parts to the document.

A] "Graphics"
B] "Styles"
C] "Pictures"
D] "Themes"

INDUSTRIAL TRAINING INSTITUTE

Monthly Test-7, Marks- 20, Date:- ______________

(Every Question Carry Two Marks)

Q.36. "............" contains commands for opening, saving, printing, and closing a file.

A] "View" tab
B] "Office Button"
C] "Insert" tab
D] "Review" tab

Q.39. The text that appears in the top margin of the page is called the ....

A] Footer
B] Column
C] Header
D] Paragraph

Q.42. To stop the automatic relative cell references, i.e. to make the cell reference absolute, type a .... character before the column and row number.

A] # hash.
B] $ dollar.
C] % percent.
D] * star.

Q.5. "..............." refer to a ready-to-use picture.

A] "WordArt"

B] "ClipArt"

C] "SmartArt"

D] "Autoshape"

Q.8. The "............." tab contains tools that controls how to slide show is presented.

A] "Design"

B] "Slide Show"

C] "Review"

D] "View"

Q.10. .... which displays icon that represent commonly used commands such as Save, Undo, and Redo.

A] Home Button

B] The Ribbon

C] The Quick Access Tool bar

D] The Office Button

Q.11. A "..........." is a connection to a location in the current documnet, another document or a website.

A] Highlink

B] hipolink

C] linkage

D] hyperlink

Q.12. .... are used to create slide shows on the computer

A] Presentation graphics

B] Analytical development programs

C] Super Slide packages

D] Slide maker tools

Q.15. In graphic presentation, programmes each presentation is divided into ....

A] charts

B] slides

C] tables

D] pictures

Q.19. A "..............." is a pre-designed presentation designed for common purpose such as photo album or a quiz show.

A] "Chart"

B] "Table"

C] "Slide"

D] "Template"

INDUSTRIAL TRAINING INSTITUTE

Monthly Test-8, Marks- 20, Date:- ______________

(Every Question Carry Two Marks)

Q.43. A primary key must be

A] Unique But Permit Null.

B] Unique and Not Null.

C] Non-unique And Not Null.

D] Non-unique And Permit Null.

Q.44. which of the following are functions performed by a DBA?

A] Database Design.

B] System Security.

C] Backup and Recovery.

D] All of the above.

Q.45. "..........." is a relation database management application that is used to create and analyze a database.

A] Word 2007.

B] Access 2007.

C] System Security.

D] PowerPoint 2007.

Q.47. A "............" is a field or set of fields in your table that provide Access with a unique identifier for every record.

A] Password.

B] Special Code.

C] Primary Key.

D] Unique Code.

Q.51. what is the first step of defining a database.

A] Designing the database.

B] Collection of data.

C] Planning your database.

D] Digitizing your data.

Q.54. DBMS means..................

A] Database Management System.

B] Domain Management System.

C] Domain Manangeemt Server.

D] Domain Management Style.

Q.58 You can enter up to charactess in a text field.

A] 375

B] 125

C] 235

D] 255

Q.1. Netscape Navigator is a type of ....

A] Utility Program.

B] Operating System.

C] Browser.

D] Web Authoring Program.

Q.2. When you type an address such as "http://www.mkcl.org", in this .org indicates.

A] Original Web Site.

B] Commercial Web Site.

C] Organizational Web Site.

D] Educational Web Site.

Q.3. You can search the World Wide Web for a specific topic by using .... and.................

A] Gophers, Fido's.

B] Scanner, Search Engine.

C] Search Engines, Indexes.

D] Browsers, Larkers.

INDUSTRIAL TRAINING INSTITUTE

Monthly Test-9, Marks- 20, Date:- ______________

(Every Question Carry Two Marks)

Q.9. The network connecting several computers all over the world is?

A] Intranet.

B] Internet.

C] Arpanet.

D] Network.

Q.10. Which of the following is a browser.

A] Web site.

B] Microsoft.

C] Internet Explorer.

D] www.

Q.11. The terms DNS stands for.

A] Data Naming System.

B] Do Name System.

C] Domain Name System.

D] Duplicate Name System.

Q.12. Internet e-mail address is .... for every user.

A] Unique.

B] Same.

C] Common.

D] None of these.

Q.13. For navigating any website, user has to enter

A] URL.

B] www.

C] PPP.

D] None of these.

Q.14. What is the full form of E-Commerce ?

A] English Commerce.

B] Electronic Commerce.

C] Electric Commerce.

D] Element Commerce.

Q.15. To send e-mail to someone you need ....

A] Resident Address.

B] Internet Connectivity.

C] Fax Address.

D] None of these.

Q.16. .... is used to see the web page.

A] Inbox.

B] Recycle bin.

C] Internet Explorer.

D] Network Neighbourhood.

Q.17. Full form of URL

A] Universal Resource Locator.

B] Uniform Resource Locator.

C] Uni Resource Locator.

D] None of these.

Q.19. Which of the following is a search engine.

A] Google.

B] Alta Vista.

C] Yahoo.

D] All of these.

INDUSTRIAL TRAINING INSTITUTE

Monthly Test-10, Marks- 20, Date:- ______________

(Every Question Carry Two Marks)

2] <b> tag makes the enclosed text bold] What is other tag to make text bold?

a] <strong>

b] <dar>

c] <black>

d] <emp>

3] Tags and test that are not directly displayed on the page are written in _____ section]

a] <html>

b] <head>

c] <title>

d] <body>

4] Which tag inserts a line horizontally on your web page?

a] <hr>

b] <line>

c] <line direction="horizontal">

d] <tr>

5] What should be the first tag in any HTML document?

a] <head>

b] <title>

c] <html>

d] <document>

6] Which tag allows you to add a row in a table?

a] <td> and </td>

b] <cr> and </cr>

c] <th> and </th>

d] <tr> and </tr>

7] How can you make a bulleted list?

a] <list>

b] <nl>

c] <ul>

d] <ol>

8] How can you make a numbered list?

a] <dl>

b] <ol>

c] <list>

d] <ul>

9] How can you make an e-mail link?

a] <a href="xxx@yyy">

b] <mail href="xxx@yyy">

c] <mail>xxx@yyy</mail>

d] <a href="mailto:xxx@yyy">

10] What is the correct HTML for making a hyperlink?

a] <a href="http:// mcqsets]com">ICT Trends Quiz</a>

b] <a name="http://mcqsets]com">ICT Trends Quiz</a>

c] <http://mcqsets]com</a>

d] url="http://mcqsets]com">ICT Trends Quiz

11] Choose the correct HTML tag to make a text italic

a] <ii>

b] <italics>

c] <italic>

d] <i>

INDUSTRIAL TRAINING INSTITUTE

Monthly Test-11, Marks- 20, Date:- ______________

(Every Question Carry Two Marks)

1] Why so JavaScript and Java have similar name?

A] JavaScript is a stripped-down version of Java

B] JavaScript's syntax is loosely based on Java's

C] They both originated on the island of Java

D] None of the above

2] When a user views a page containing a JavaScript program, which machine actually executes the script?

A] The User's machine running a Web browser

B] The Web server

C] A central machine deep within Netscape's corporate offices

D] None of the above

3] _______ JavaScript is also called client-side JavaScript]

A] Microsoft

B] Navigator

C] LiveWire

D] Native

4] ___________ JavaScript is also called server-side JavaScript]

A] Microsoft

B] Navigator

C] LiveWire

D] Native

5] What are variables used for in JavaScript Programs?

A] Storing numbers, dates, or other values

B] Varying randomly

C] Causing high-school algebra flashbacks

D] None of the above

6] ______ JavaScript statements embedded in an HTML page can respond to user events such as mouse-clicks, form input, and page navigation]

A] Client-side

B] Server-side

C] Local

D] Native

7] What should appear at the very end of your JavaScript?

The <script LANGUAGE="JavaScript">tag

A] The </script>

B] The <script>

C] The END statement

D] None of the above

8] Which of the following can't be done with client-side JavaScript?

A] Validating a form

B] Sending a form's contents by email

C] Storing the form's contents to a database file on the server

D] None of the above

9] Which of the following are capabilities of functions in JavaScript?

A] Return a value

B] Accept parameters and Return a value

C] Accept parameters

D] None of the above

10] Which of the following is not a valid JavaScript variable name?

A] 2names

B] _first_and_last_names

C] FirstAndLast

D] None of the above

INDUSTRIAL TRAINING INSTITUTE

Monthly Test-12, Marks- 20, Date:- ______________

(Every Question Carry Two Marks)

Q. 1 ________ is the practice and precautions taken to protect valuable information from unauthorized access, recording, disclosure or destruction.

A] Network Security
B] Database Security
C] Information Security
D] Physical Security

Q. 2 _______ platforms are used for safety and protection of information in the cloud.

A] Cloud workload protection platforms
B] Cloud security protocols
C] AWS
D] One Drive

Q. 3 Compromising confidential information comes under__

A] Bug
B] Threat
C] Vulnerability
D] Attack

Q. 4 An attempt to harm, damage or cause threat to a system or network is broadly termed as ______

A] Cyber-crime
B] Cyber Attack
C] System hijacking
D] Digital crime

Q. 5 The CIA triad is often represented by which of the following?

A] Triangle
B] Diagonal
C] Ellipse
D] Circle

Q. 6 Related to information security, confidentiality is the opposite of which of the following?

A] Closure
B] Disclosure
C] Disaster
D] Disposal

Q. 8 _______ means the protection of data from modification by unknown users.

A] Confidentiality
B] Integrity
C] Authentication
D] Non-repudiation

Q. 9 ________ of information means, only authorized users are capable of accessing the information.

A] Confidentiality

B] Integrity

C] Non-repudiation

D] Availability

Q. 10 This helps in identifying the origin of information and authentic user. This referred to here as ____________

A] Confidentiality

B] Integrity

C] Authenticity

D] Availability

Q. 11 Data _____________ is used to ensure confidentiality.

A] Encryption

B] Locking

C] Decryption

D] Backup

www.ingramcontent.com/pod-product-compliance
Ingram Content Group UK Ltd.
Pitfield, Milton Keynes, MK11 3LW, UK
UKHW021909190726
13853UKWH00002B/595